Energizing STAFF Meetings

Energizing STAFF Meetings

SHEILA ELLER & JOHN ELLER

CORWIN PRESS
A SAGE Publications Company
Thousand Oaks, California

For information:

Corwin Press
A Sage Publications Company
2455 Teller Road
Thousand Oaks, California 91320
www.corwinpress.com

Sage Publications Ltd
1 Oliver's Yard
55 City Road
London EC1Y 1SP
United Kingdom

Sage Publications India Pvt. Ltd.
B-42, Panchsheel Enclave
Post Box 4109
New Delhi 110 017 India

Printed in the United States of America

Library of Congress Cataloging-in-Publication Data

Eller, Sheila.
Energizing staff meetings / Sheila Eller and John Eller.
    p. cm.
Includes bibliographical references and index.
ISBN 1-4129-2432-4 (cloth) — ISBN 1-4129-2433-2 (pbk.)
  1. School management and organization. 2. Meetings. 3. Teacher-principal relationships. 4. Educational leadership. I. Eller, John, 1957- II. Title.
LB2806.E463 2006
371.2'03—dc22

                                  2005023352

This book is printed on acid-free paper.

05   06   07   08   09   10   9   8   7   6   5   4   3   2   1

Acquisitions Editor:	Jean Ward
Editorial Assistant:	Jordan Barbakow
Production Editor:	Kristen Gibson
Copy Editor:	Freelance Editorial Services
Typesetter:	C&M Digitals (P) Ltd.
Indexer:	Terri Corry
Proofreader:	Ellen Brink
Cover Designer:	Tracy Miller

Contents

Preface

The Challenges of Energizing Staff Meetings

In schools today, we face challenges and opportunities. Many teachers report that children have changed and teaching has become more challenging over the years. Some parents have increased their demands on schools and teachers. School budgets have been flat or have decreased, even though accountability standards have increased. With all of these and other pressures faced by schools recently, it is easy to see why some staff members have become disheartened with their work. When the adults in a school have negative feelings about their jobs, these emotions can be transferred to the students; this only makes matters worse.

Effective school leaders have learned that it is important to work with their teachers to energize their work environment. One area in which leaders can have a positive impact is the organization and operation of staff meetings. That is the focus of this book.

Many of us who are currently in or are getting ready to assume leadership positions were not necessarily exposed to energized staff meetings ourselves; we have had to learn strategies and adapt them to fit the needs of our teachers. This book is dedicated to those leaders who want to move beyond the leadership experiences of the past and provide their teachers with energized and motivating settings. Negative emotions can be transmitted across multiple levels in an organization, and so can positive feelings. The positive ideas that you use in your staff meetings will help to establish and nurture the kinds of positive emotions that your teachers will need to stay motivated and focused in their work with students.

As you read this book, you will notice that it has been designed in a slightly different manner than an instructional manual. The main focus of this book is activities that you can use or adapt in working with your teachers. Although there is background information that is needed to understand the context of the strategies, we have tried to condense it so that it can be read and understood quickly.

The real details come in the descriptions of the activities. In writing these, we tried to be as detailed as possible so that you can read and immediately implement them in your setting. Many of the activities come from the workshops we have done with school leaders and other professionals over the years. Others have been implemented by one of us in schools, staff development sessions, presentations, facilitation experiences, graduate coursework, and other development activities. Some of the activities have appeared in other books that we have used as research for our professional practice. We have tried to give credit to everyone who has shared some of their wisdom with us over the years.

When considering implementing the activities and ideas contained in this book, keep several things in mind. First, make sure that you try to match the right activity to the needs of your teachers. Second, be sure that the strategies you are considering fit in with your level of comfort and strength areas. Finally, be sure to debrief with staff members after each activity is completed. By debriefing, you ensure that their minds are able to interact with the information they just learned. Also, you can help them begin to develop generalizations and understandings that will go far beyond the staff meeting where they experienced the activity.

The debriefing serves another important function: It helps teachers to transfer the positive emotions that they experienced in the meeting to other settings, such as their classrooms. We are finding that, over the years, many teachers become accustomed to feeling negative emotions in staff meetings and do not notice the positive aspects of a meeting at first unless someone either points them out or helps them to see these positives. Without this awareness, they may just go back into their classrooms and continue the same old behaviors. If this happens, teachers miss a major purpose of the time and energy you spend to energize their staff meetings. Debriefing and helping teachers to draw out their conclusions about the energizing activities increases the chances that they will take not only the activity back to their classrooms but also a positive attitude.

We hope you find this book as helpful to read as we have found it fun to write. As with any book of this nature, it is a work in progress. As we work with more schools and school leaders, we will keep adding to our professional knowledge base, just as you will as you implement some of the ideas and strategies in your own setting.

We would like to hear your ideas and suggestions. Please feel free to contact us at any time with your ideas, questions, or feedback about the activities and ideas that we have provided you. You can reach us at seller3600@aol.com (Sheila) or jellerthree@aol.com (John).

We wish you success in your efforts to energize your staff members; enjoy the journey and give yourself a chance to grow and learn as you take on this challenging and rewarding journey—a journey toward an energized staff.

—Sheila and John Eller

The business of leaders, of heroes, is tricky. Leadership is not something that is done to people, like fixing your teeth. Leadership is unlocking people's potential to become better.

—Former U.S. Senator Bill Bradley

CORWIN PRESS

The Corwin Press logo—a raven striding across an open book—represents the union of courage and learning. Corwin Press is committed to improving education for all learners by publishing books and other professional development resources for those serving the field of PreK–12 education. By providing practical, hands-on materials, Corwin Press continues to carry out the promise of its motto: **"Helping Educators Do Their Work Better."**

About the Authors

Sheila Eller has worked in a multitude of educational settings during her career. In addition to her current position as a principal in the Stillwater, Minnesota, School District, she also has served as a principal in other schools in Minnesota and Illinois, as a university professor, as a special education teacher, as a Title I math teacher, and as a self-contained classroom teacher in Grades 1–4. She is a member of the executive board of the Minnesota Association for Supervision and Curriculum Development (ASCD) and has been a regional president of the Minnesota Association of Elementary School Principals. She has completed advanced coursework in educational administration and supervision at St. Cloud State University and holds a master's degree from Creighton University in Omaha, Nebraska, and a bachelor's degree from Iowa State University.

Ms. Eller is a regular presenter at the ASCD national conventions, sharing her expertise on the topic of effective staff meetings and multiage instruction. While serving as a professor at National-Louis University in Evanston, Illinois, she worked on the development team for a classroom mathematics series that was adopted by several districts in the region. Her classroom and instructional techniques were featured in a video that was produced as a complement to this series. She works with educators to develop energized staff meetings, school improvement initiatives, multiage teaching strategies, employee supervision, and other teaching and learning content areas.

John Eller has had a variety of experiences working with adults during his years in education. He has worked with graduate students to develop professional learning communities; served as the executive director of the Minnesota Association for Supervision and Curriculum Development; worked as a principals' training center director; held a position as an assistant superintendent for curriculum, learning, and staff development; and held several principal positions in Iowa and Illinois. In addition to the work he does in training and supporting facilitators, he also works in the areas of dealing with difficult people; building professional learning communities; employee evaluation; conferencing skills; coaching skills; strategic planning strategies; school improvement planning and implementation; differentiated instruction; leadership for differentiation; employee recruitme]nt, selection, and induction; supervisory skills; and effective teaching strategies.

Dr. Eller earned a PhD in educational leadership and policy studies from Loyola University Chicago and a master's degree in educational leadership from the University of Nebraska–Omaha. He has authored books on substitute teaching, wrote *The Training Video Series for the Professional School Bus Driver,* contributes articles to the publication *Superintendents Only,* and assisted in the design of the e-learning communities used at the building level for staff development. He wrote *Effective Group Facilitation in Education: How to Energize Meetings and Manage Difficult Groups,* released by Corwin Press in 2004.

1

Why Energize?

The best leaders . . . almost without exception and at every level are master users of stories and symbols.

—Tom Peters

Kevin, a middle-level principal, always dreaded getting his staff together for meetings. Most of the time, the members of his staff just sat and listened as he talked about upcoming events and tasks that needed to be tackled in his school. Sometimes, he had a hard time getting people to talk at all during his meetings. When the staff meetings were over, Kevin found that he had not solved any of the problems or issues that he had called the meeting to deal with in the first place.

His teachers also did not look forward to the meetings. Many of the staff members were open about the fact that the meetings were a waste of time. Because many of the staff members had worked with Kevin for a long time, they had resigned themselves to the fact that meetings would always be boring.

Karla, on the other hand, had a much different situation happening in her meetings. The staff members at Karla's school met regularly but for short periods of time. Each of her meetings had a clear and focused agenda. Each of her meetings started with an opening activity to connect her staff members. At the end of the meeting, strategies were normally put in place to help teachers review the accomplishments of the session. Karla helped her staff members learn how to connect emotionally and use the unique strengths and talents present in the teaching staff. Tasks were addressed and accomplished during her meetings.

In each of the preceding scenarios, a different perspective on staff meetings was illustrated. What made Kevin's meetings so ineffective, whereas Karla was able to make her meetings a place where staff members could learn to work together and solve problems as a team? In this book, we will explore the secrets of making staff meetings engaging and energizing experiences.

Good leaders know how to motivate their staff members. One effective way to motivate staff is to conduct energized staff meetings. Because of a variety of factors, many leaders find it difficult to conduct energized staff meetings. This book is designed to help school and district-level leaders to be successful in improving their meetings. In this chapter, you will learn the following:

- Reasons why leaders don't always conduct energized staff meetings
- The positive effects of energized staff meetings
- The positive effects of building a strong staff culture
- The impact of energized meetings on you, the leader
- How the information in this book can help you to improve your staff meetings

What Is an Energized, Effective Staff Meeting?

An energized, effective staff meeting is an experience in which team members are engaged and actively involved in the content and substance of the meeting. It is also a situation in which all of the minds of the staff members are connecting and working together to solve problems and to move the organization forward in its goals and objectives. An energized staff meeting may look very calm on the surface, or it may be filled with all kinds of physical and mental activities. At times, meeting leaders need to inject energizing strategies into a meeting to get people to connect and be creative, whereas in other instances, the same leaders need to provide activities and experiences that mentally engage participants in the meeting content.

Sometimes, meeting leaders get themselves into trouble because they think they need to entertain their teachers during their meetings. They feel they are a failure if people are not on the edge of their seats during the whole meeting. The need to entertain can turn some people off to the concept of energizing meetings; this can cause meeting leaders to do nothing rather than try to make their meetings more engaging.

This book was written to serve as a practical guide to help you, the meeting leader, get the minds of your staff members engaged in the meeting content. There are activities listed here that may require a group to be physically active, whereas others are more low key in nature. The ideas with less physical activity engage a group but in a different way than the more active energizers. It is up to you to decide when to use specific strategies to help your group through a particular phase or situation that they may be facing. Remember, your goal is to get their minds active and connected; how you do that in your building may be different from how others do it in their settings.

What Keeps Leaders From Conducting Energized Staff Meetings?

Discomfort With Trying New Ideas

In some instances, the leader may be reluctant to try new ideas with staff. After all, once the patterns of meeting behaviors have been set, a certain amount of comfort is established. It can be hard for some people to break out of these "normal" behaviors and try some new ideas. Implementing energizing activities takes a leader who is interested in changing the status quo. Schools can become stagnant places where people are positively reinforced for not "rocking the boat." A leader who wants to try energizing activities needs to look at the school staff members and decide that they need to be shaken up a little. To be successful in conducting energized staff meetings, the leader has to find a way to put this discomfort behind him or her and to work through new ideas. Thomas Kuhn, in his book *The Structure of Scientific Revolutions* (1996), presented a model that can be used to explain and understand the process people go through in examining new ideas or changes. The following general steps have been adapted from Kuhn's work:

- The person or group of people experience information or data.
- The mind begins to draw conclusions based on the information.
- These conclusions or generalizations continue to be strengthened until they form a way of thinking or frame of reference.
- A comfort zone is established by having a frame of reference to guide thinking on a topic or topics.
- Something in the environment changes that contradicts or challenges the person's or group's frame of reference.
- The person or group tries to justify the existing thought pattern or frame of reference by bending or changing the incoming information to fit the old thought pattern.

- After many attempts to bend or change the information, the person or group begins to see that the old way of thinking is outdated, and a new frame of reference is formed around the new ideas or information that have been picked up by the group members.
- The process remains stable until the next challenge to the new frame of reference is presented.

In essence, we all can become comfortable with the way things are going. Even when the existing state is not all that great, it is at least predictable. We may be more comfortable with a predictable situation  that is not positive than with one that holds the potential to be positive but is unknown at this time. This process can work against leaders, who may be comfortable with boring and ineffective meetings because they are predictable. They may be uncomfortable trying something new because there is some amount of uncertainty.

It is far easier to keep doing the same things, even if they don't work, than to work to implement change. Here are some strategies others have found beneficial when working through the discomfort of changing their staff meetings and implementing energizing staff meetings:

Strategies to Overcome Self-Reluctance

- Worst-case scenario analysis: Examine the worst thing that could happen as a result of trying an energizing activity. If you can live with the worst-case scenario, try the new idea.
- Best-case scenario analysis: Examine the best things that could happen as a result of trying a new, energizing activity with your staff. If the outcome is worth the effort, go ahead and give the new idea a try.
- Idea familiarization: To help you work past the "information bending" stage described previously, review the new idea or ideas several times and think about how the energizing activities could fit into your leadership behavior. This will help you work through the process of implementing a new idea and keep you from blocking the change.
- Partner assistance: Engage a partner in helping you to evaluate and implement a new idea for your staff. Asking someone to work with you will help you to productively work through the issues that normally appear as you implement new ideas or strategies.
- Staff collaboration: Many leaders enlist the help of teachers as they implement new ideas. These leaders can use the support of teacher-leaders to sell and implement new ideas. Consider how one leader we recently worked with used staff member support and expertise to implement a new meeting strategy.

After seeing that his staff needed to find ways to work together more productively, Rod formed a committee to study the problem. At their first meeting, the teachers on the committee told Rod that the staff meetings were not seen as productive. Rod asked the teachers to suggest ideas for changing staff meetings. Several of the staff members suggested that openers be used to get the meetings started in a productive manner. Three teachers volunteered to introduce the concept of openers at the next staff meeting.

At the next meeting, these teachers presented the idea of implementing openers. Several teachers expressed concerns about the process, but in general, the staff agreed that having opening activities at their staff meetings could be good. Rod was able to move the concept forward without putting himself out on a limb. The small group of teachers was able to take the initial "heat" for the new idea while helping to move it forward. If Rod had been seen as the initiator of the idea, he may have run into resistance.

Negative Staff Reactions

Leaders are not the only people in schools who are reluctant to try new ideas; teachers also don't like to move out of their comfort zones. At times, this reluctance can be quite strong. People may exhibit very negative behaviors to get a leader to move back into their comfort zone. They are good at figuring out the "threshold of pain" a leader will tolerate before he or she gives up on an idea and moves back on the plan to conduct energizing staff meetings. If the teachers know that their negative attitudes may cause the leader to abandon a new idea, they will do whatever they can to make the new idea fail. Negative behaviors may range from simple eye rolling to observable defiance of the new strategies. John recently had such an experience with a group of office workers who showed defiance in engaging in team-building activities.

As John was explaining that the office workers needed to get to know each other and build collaborative relationships, several of them looked at each other in disgust. They were rolling their eyes, and several made jokes about the activity that was being proposed. John suspended his judgment of their comments and had everyone meet in the hall. After he started the activity, one of the more abrasive members of the group said, "I am not doing this activity." John said, "OK, just follow along with the rest of us."

As the group moved through the activity, it was obvious the negative person looked foolish just walking along. In a minute or so, she grabbed onto one the ropes for the device that the group was moving. John made no comment, and the other office workers didn't say anything to her as well. After the activity was over, she waited around until the other employees left. She said to John, "In the future, please let me know what you are planning to do, so I can get myself ready." John agreed to do that. He offered her a chance to be involved in the planning committee for future activities; she agreed and became a supporter of future activities.

Although this story may seem too good to be true, by allowing this worker some space, she was able to work through her negative feelings about participating. In this case, if John had made a big deal out of her comment about not participating, she would have resisted. If John had become more forceful in getting her to engage, a small battle could have erupted. The staff members may have backed her, and the situation easily could have gotten out of control. In this case, by not making a big deal out of her resistance, John was able to help her work through it. Because he knew the personality of the office worker, he knew how to handle the situation.

Here are some strategies and techniques that you may consider using when facing reluctant staff members. Remember that it is crucial for you to evaluate the situation before selecting a strategy to deal with it.

Techniques to Deal with Negative Staff Reactions

- Practice suspension of opinion.

    A good technique to use in dealing with staff reluctance is the suspension of opinion. With this skill, you control your inner feelings of anxiety and ignore the eye rolling and negative comments. This can be a hard skill to learn and implement, but it also can be highly effective in dealing with negative emotions. With the suspension of opinion, it is important for you to believe that implementing energizing activities will be good for your teachers. Suspension is based on the reinforcement theory of extinction: What you ignore will go away. At times, we have seen leaders and staff members get into arguments right in the middle of a staff meeting because the leader decided to respond to a negative comment made by a staff member.

    As you get ready to implement energizing activities with your staff, think through all of the possible negative comments you may get and who you think may make them. This will help you to ignore the comments and move your group forward.

- Explain the reasons for doing the activities.

  As with any new practice, it is important to explain to your staff members why you are implementing it in their staff meetings. Be sure to talk about the benefits that your teachers will gain as a result of getting more engaged and involved in the staff meetings. Let them know that you want to make their meetings a place where everyone can feel comfortable and share in generating solutions to the problems the school faces. Finally, be sure to tell them that you want them to have some fun in their meetings. Implementing energizing activities will enable them to have some fun and learn at the same time.

- Ask the staff to list their concerns; address these concerns.

  Sometimes, teachers may have legitimate concerns about getting involved in more energizing and engaging staff meetings. Some of your teachers may have experienced some of the self-awareness activities so famous during earlier times in education. Although many of these programs were good at what they were trying to accomplish, others were not followed up in any systematic manner. Other staff members may have legitimate concerns about the types of activities you are proposing. Some of your teachers may even have health concerns that need to be taken into account.

If you believe there are concerns that need to be addressed in the group before moving on with energizing activities, be sure to hold an open meeting to get those concerns out and addressed before moving forward. See how one principal, Carol, conducted her meeting to make sure that all of the staff concerns about her new ideas for staff meetings were addressed.

Right after she explained that the basic structure for staff meetings was going to change, Carol told the teachers that she wanted to hear their concerns about the new idea. She divided the teachers into groups of five and asked them to work together to generate a list of concerns about implementing energizing activities in future meetings. She also asked them to talk about the ways that these concerns could be overcome. Finally, she told the small groups that she wanted them to generate a list of possible benefits to the staff that implementing energizing activities could bring. After about 10 minutes, she had each team report its findings. Several legitimate concerns were brought out, but other teams had solutions for these concerns. In the end, the teachers saw that their concerns had been addressed in a positive and energizing manner. The new meeting activities were well received.

Embed Positive Statements to
Help Frame the Thinking of Group Members

As the leader, your attitude goes a long way toward framing the thought patterns of your teachers. If you approach the new activities with excitement and interest, they will fall in line as well. You can embed positive statements into your introduction of the activities that will set the stage for their success. Here are some statements that you may find helpful as you introduce new energizing activities:

Helpful Introductory Statements

- You are really going to learn a lot about our group as we . . .
- The next activity will help you to . . .
- As we get ready to move into . . . be sure to think about how it can help us work together better as a team.
- You will really like . . .
- As you work together in teams during the next activity, be sure to look for . . .
- This is going to be fun and help you learn . . .
- Because you have done so well working together in the past, we will move to the next level . . .
- To energize our thinking and problem-solving skills today . . .
- As you get into your problem-solving groups . . .

At times, we apologize for allowing our teachers to work together effectively and experience good staff meetings. Here are some examples that tend to "turn off" the thinking of staff members and make them feel negative about their participation in activities:

**Introductory Statements That Negatively
Frame the Thoughts of Meeting Participants**

- I know that you have some concerns about participating today in . . .
- You may not want to do this, but . . .
- This may seem goofy to you . . .
- In the past, we have had bad experiences with this type of activity, but . . .
- I am sure that you will not want to do this . . .
- The last time we tried this, several of you giggled . . .
- You probably don't want to do this, but . . .

As you read these statements, you may be thinking, "Why would anyone say these kinds of things when introducing activities?" Believe it or not, we find these kinds of statements to be very common with leaders and their teachers. Some leaders are not even aware they are saying them until we point it out to them. The most common reason leaders make these negative statements is nervousness. Think through how you plan to introduce the use of energizing activities so that you can frame them as positive rather than negative. With careful planning, you can avoid making mistakes by "winging" the introductory section of the meeting and possibly turning people off by making inappropriate statements.

Lack of Knowledge or Strategies

In the typical administrator or leader training session, very little information is provided about energizing staff meetings. Because most leaders have not been exposed to this type of training, it is not surprising that leaders have limited knowledge about this topic. This book has been developed as a guide to help you learn and implement energizing activities with your teachers.

Positive Impacts of Energized Meetings on Staff, School Climate, and Culture

Energizing activities have positive effects on staff members. This section describes some of the major positive impacts of energized staff meetings.

Promotes Good Feelings About Meetings

Implementing energizing activities helps to build good feelings about staff meetings. People begin to look forward to having some fun and getting their work accomplished when they know that energizing activities are being implemented.

Creates Favorable Impressions of the Leader

Like it or not, many of your staff members see you in limited situations. Because you are involved in a variety of activities throughout the day, your teachers' perceptions of your leadership abilities are based on seeing you in a variety of limited situations. The staff meeting time you have set aside may be the longest amount of uninterrupted time your staff members have with you. If your meetings are energetic and engaging, your teachers will perceive you as effective; if not, they will begin to think that you are not a good leader.

Models Effective Behaviors for Teachers

Our teachers learn a lot by following the examples of others. If your run boring, dull meetings yet tell them they need to engage their students in interesting instruction, you are communicating mixed messages to them. If, on the other hand, your teachers see you challenging them by conducting productive and energized staff meetings, they will begin to see what you mean. The old phrase "a picture is worth a thousand words" applies here.

In addition to implementing good, on-track energizing activities, it is important that you take the time to point out what you are doing in your staff meetings and why you are implementing these activities. These explanations don't need to be long to be effective. See how the leader in the following example points out why the teachers are engaging in an energizing activity:

It is important that we focus on the positive aspects of our school in order to grow and learn as a staff. We are going to use a technique called "Good News" to open our meeting. In small groups of six, I want each of you to share something good that happened to you in relation to our school during the last month. After you are finished, I want you to be ready to share two or three of the Good News items you heard with the entire faculty.

In this case, the principal asked the teachers to talk about a positive event related to their work in the school. The purpose of this activity was to help teachers begin to draw out the good things about the school in order to build a positive culture. She summed up that outcome in her introductory statement. If the principal models positive talk, then teachers will follow along and begin to do the same.

The idea of modeling effective behaviors is a topic that may require more information than the scope of this book allows, but in general, teachers look to you, the leader, to show them what you mean. Implementing energizing activities provides the perfect vehicle for doing this with your teachers.

Gives Teachers Strategies to Try in Their Classrooms

Implementing energizing activities can also give teachers ideas for activities that they can use in their classrooms. In our work with teacher groups, we have found that people are hungry for ideas and strategies that they can use in their classrooms. Today's teachers are looking for ways to help students break down communication barriers and work together as a learning community. The energizers that you use at your staff meetings can be easily adapted for use in classrooms of every level. Some leaders take the time to point out how these strategies can be implemented in classrooms, whereas others ask the teachers to take a few minutes at the end of an activity to talk about how the idea or strategy could be used in their classrooms. See how Julie, the principal of a middle school, involved her staff members in thinking about how an activity could be used with their students:

We have been working in our school to help our students see how they can help each other out. Take a minute to talk in pairs about how you think we could adapt the activity that we just finished, Toxic Waste Transfer, to help our houses learn how to work together.

By asking the teachers to generate ideas, Julie helped them to personalize the strategy and develop their own ideas. They were more invested in the idea than if Julie had said, "This is a great idea, you all need to use it with your students." Julie could have provided more assistance to her staff members by offering to make some Toxic Waste Transfer kits or by purchasing the materials for those interested in making their own kits.

Builds Collegiality and Community

Obviously, once people are allowed to work together and interact, the level of collegiality will increase. When implementing energizing activities, it is crucial that you have people work in groups that vary in membership. Most of the energizing activities highlighted in this book require teachers to get to know their colleagues in a deeper and more meaningful way. Collegiality and community can be built through this higher level of knowledge and understanding. Be sure to watch how your teachers interact as you continue to implement energizing activities with them. You will see an increased level of understanding of one another and more collegiality as they work together.

Helps People Deal With Negative Situations in a Positive Manner

When your teachers are engaged in energized staff meetings, they can see things in a different light and begin to look for positive resolutions to problems. As we have worked with faculty groups, we have noticed that through the implementation of energizing activities, teachers become better at solving problems. When energizing problem-solving strategies are used, more people are involved in developing solutions to problems. The expectation that all staff members have a stake in solving problems evolves as a result of energized staff meetings. Many of the activities presented in this book work toward getting everyone involved in positive problem resolution.

Gives People Some Sense of Control Over Their Environment

Teachers sometimes feel they have little or no control over their work environment. The schedule is established for them, their students are determined in advance, and the principal tells them what they can and can't do. By conducting staff meetings that are more interactive and energizing, some of the control over the workplace is given back to the teachers. In some of the schools in which we have helped staff members learn how to work together in energized staff meetings, the teachers have actually been placed in charge of implementing those changes. By being in charge of their own activities, teachers gain some control over their environment. This can be a very motivating and exciting prospect for teachers.

In addition to giving people control over their environment, we have seen some very innovative activities develop when teachers are put in charge of generating the energizing activities. In two groups we recently worked with, a small subgroup was given the assignment to start each meeting by introducing an energizer. People looked forward to these energizers, and because the staff members were responsible for generating the ideas, the other teachers were receptive to the activities that were presented. The staff members told us that they felt they were in control of a part of the agenda; this is one of the reasons we had asked staff members to generate energizers in the first place.

The Impact of Energized Meetings on You, the Leader

You Look Forward to Meetings

Leaders who implement energizing activities seem to become energized themselves. These leaders actually begin to look forward to meetings rather than see them as negative experiences. It is exciting to watch your staff members have fun and work together. Your staff meetings become places where real solutions to problems emerge rather than places for people to complain. The time you allot for your staff meetings seems to fly by when you have people engaged in exciting and energizing activities. In general, you will look forward to meeting and working with your teachers in your meetings as a result of implementing energizing activities.

You Are Motivated and Energized

Implementing energizing activities also rubs off on the leader. Many leaders will join in the activities that they ask their teachers to participate in during staff meetings. If you do join in, you will feel the increased energy that your staff members are experiencing. Even if you don't join in right away, you will enjoy watching your staff members get excited during your meetings. This can be energizing in itself. Let yourself go and allow the newfound energy to influence you as well as your teachers.

You See the Positive Impact of Your Leadership on Staff Members

Most of us get into leadership positions to help people grow and learn. If you implement energizing activities with your teachers, you will immediately see the results of your leadership efforts. This instant feedback tends to motivate school leaders and reminds them that their primary job is to be the "lead teacher" of the teachers. A motivated staff, in turn, will do a better job with the children—the real reason we are in this business in the first place.

How to Use This Book to Improve Your Staff Meetings

This book was written as a guide for you to use in your quest to add energy to your staff meetings. The activities listed here have been successfully implemented in a variety of settings in schools and educational organizations around the country. Each of the leaders who has tried these ideas has taken the unique needs and characteristics of his or her staff into account before putting these ideas into practice. Make sure that you carefully read through the descriptions and the background information for each activity and then evaluate how the technique may work in your particular situation. The context for each activity is important to your success in implementing it.

Also, keep in mind the readiness level of your teachers for energizing activities. Like any new idea, you will need to build up their readiness and understanding with simple, easy-to-implement activities before moving to more complex ideas. Move your staff along at a pace that is comfortable for them to ensure success.

This book has been designed to provide you with activities that you may find helpful at different stages in the meeting process. In Chapter 2, "Barriers to Good Staff Meetings and How to Overcome Them," you will learn how to deal with the most common problems that get in the way of implementing energized staff meeting activities. In Chapter 3, "Great Beginnings," you will learn how to start off an energized staff meeting on the right foot. Chapter 4, "Keeping the Group Engaged," will help you maintain the energy level throughout the meeting. Chapter 5, "Building on the Positive Emotional Connections of Staff Members," will provide ideas and techniques to help you further your work in developing a collaborative community of teachers by using emotionally based energizers to connect your teachers in a powerful way.

The information contained in Chapter 6, "Extended Meetings . . . When You Have More Time," has been selected for use in meetings that go beyond the normal hour to hour and a half that is set aside for most staff meetings. Many leaders find that these longer meetings involve staff development or opening-day sessions and provide a challenge to keeping people energized and connected. Closing down a meeting in an energizing manner is the topic of Chapter 7, "Closing the Meeting With a Bang," which will provide you with the ideas you need to ensure that the energy you have worked to build during the entire meeting is not lost at the very end. People always remember the beginning and the end, so we want to make sure that they will remember that your meeting ended in a positive and energized manner.

Finally, Chapter 8, "Closing Thoughts and Next Steps," will sum up the information presented in this book and give you practical ideas about how to move forward in your efforts to engage your staff members in energized meetings.

Summary

In this chapter, you began your journey on the rewarding road to energizing your staff meetings and helping your staff to grow and learn. As you can see from your reading, the effects of energizing your staff meetings are positive and worth the effort. Conducting energized staff meetings not only makes the meeting experience more fun and rewarding but also helps to build the collegiality and collaborative skills of your participants.

As you will see in Chapter 2, there are many barriers that can work against you and undermine your efforts to energize your staff meetings. With the information that you will learn in the next chapter, you will be armed to deal with these barriers and to turn your staff meetings into productive and positive experiences for you and the staff you lead.

2

Barriers to Good Staff Meetings and How to Overcome Them

Success is to be measured not so much by the position that one has reached in life as by the obstacles that one has overcome while trying to succeed.

—Booker T. Washington

There are barriers that work against our best efforts to make meetings good experiences for those who attend them. Some of these barriers occur naturally, whereas others are built by the organization or its members. In this chapter, we will examine the most common barriers and ways to overcome them to ensure energized staff meetings. You will learn the following:

- The most common barriers to energized staff meetings and their causes
- Strategies to identify barriers

- Techniques to deal with barriers to good staff meetings, either in the planning or meeting-delivery process
- Ways to engage participants to become active partners in eliminating barriers to energized meetings

Common Barriers and Their Causes

Although meetings are commonplace in our society, they aren't always productive uses of our time. Often, there are barriers that get in the way of successful meetings. Some of the more common barriers that may negatively impact your meetings are described in this section.

Not Enough Time Devoted to the Meeting or to Important Topics

A common barrier to meeting effectiveness is that there is not enough time for the meeting or inadequate time has been set aside to address important topics. Consider the following example of this barrier in action:

Ted, a building-level principal, schedules a 30-minute staff meeting each week. He cannot hold this meeting for longer than 30 minutes because of a contractual clause. He has been asked by his superintendent to work with the staff to develop a set of recommendations for how the district's Partnership Program should allocate its grant award for the next school year. This agenda item is one of several that need to be addressed during the 30-minute meeting. His staff has just gotten started with the discussion of the grant-award process when the 30-minute time limit is reached. People begin to leave the meeting, and the agenda item cannot be addressed.

Ways to Deal With This Barrier

Here are some ideas that others have found beneficial in eliminating this barrier:

- Write the amount time that is to be devoted to each item on the agenda during the meeting; help the group stay on schedule.
- Appoint a staff member to serve as a timekeeper and notify the group when it needs to move on to other agenda topics.

- Hold a special meeting that deals just with an important topic.
- At the beginning of the meeting, alert staff members that an important topic needs their consideration and ask whether all other agenda items can be removed to provide the time needed to address the issue.
- Rearrange the agenda so that the most important items come first; if time runs out, less important items can be handled quickly or addressed at a future meeting.
- Make a yearlong calendar and plot the most important events that need teacher consideration and the months these items need to be addressed; plan agendas using this calendar.
- Take informational or routine business items off the agenda. If they can be handled using another more efficient method, use that medium to get the message to faculty. Consider placing such items in an announcement flyer or sending them by e-mail or some other method so that they don't take up valuable meeting time.

Too Much Time Devoted to the Meeting or to One Topic

We all have been in situations in which an idea or concept has been talked about too much. Most people would like to have a balance between thorough discussion of a topic and its quick resolution. When the same topic appears on the agenda at several consecutive meetings, it starts to get stale. If your topics are stale, you will have trouble energizing your meetings even if you use a variety of the activities illustrated in this book. As you begin to think about improving the quality of your meetings, be sure to take a close look at the topics you typically discuss. If they seem worn out, consider finding a way to deal with them outside your normal meeting structure.

Ways to Deal With This Barrier

This barrier is related to the previous idea, failing to provide adequate time for the meeting agenda. Here are some ideas you may find helpful when you see that an agenda item is taking more than its share of time during a meeting or series of meetings:

- Tell the group you believe the agenda item is taking too much time; solicit feedback from meeting participants about their perceptions of the situation.
- Set a time limit for the continued discussion and resolution of the agenda item that is taking too much time or energy.

- Ask the group to discuss whether the time being spent on this item is helping to resolve the issue or whether it is just giving them a chance to vent their frustrations.
- Develop a visual representation or map of the situation to help the group see the complexities of its resolution; use this visual representation or map to help the group design a process for solving the problem this agenda item presents to the group and its meeting effectiveness.
- Summarize how much time has already been spent talking about the agenda item; help the group to see how it has kept them from addressing other important issues.
- Break complex agenda items into parts; discuss parts of larger items over several meetings or sessions.
- If you are not able to move the discussion of an item forward, table it until another meeting date. Establish a clear follow-up schedule and help the group develop a strategy to move the item toward its final resolution.
- Hold a special meeting at which a large or time-consuming agenda item is the major point of discussion.
- Identify the major points of a complex item and have small task forces work on those points; ask them to report their progress at the next meeting.

Lack of Urgency About the Meeting Content

Another common barrier to energized meetings is a lack of urgency about the topic or topics of discussion. If participants do not see the resolution of topics as important or urgent, they will have trouble putting their emotions and energy behind them. At times, staff members may be asked to talk about subjects they have no direct interest in talking about. If this is the case, it will be very difficult to build energy.

At times, a topic may not seem directly related to staff members, but when it is examined deeper, it becomes clear that its resolution will have an impact on the meeting participants. In these cases, it is the job of the meeting leader to help participants make a clear connection to the topic. In the following example, read how Sharon, the leader of the meeting, tied the topic to the interests and needs of the participants:

Today we need to talk about the district's policy on hazing. On the surface, it may seem this policy only relates to high school students. Recently, several elementary schools have experienced situations in which school employees have been held responsible for situations when playground hazing was taking place but nobody on duty did anything about it. As we read through the policy materials, think about how the general statements may apply to us here at Washington School.

In this example, the principal told the teachers how looking at the hazing policy could help them to avoid troubles in the future. She also involved the staff in a meaningful way when she asked them to note statements that could apply to the school. Even though this example is simple, it illustrates that energizing meetings don't have to involve complex activities. You can energize a meeting by getting your teachers' minds engaged in processing during a meeting.

Ways to Deal With This Barrier

Dealing with a lack of urgency can be difficult to address, but here are some ideas that others have used to successfully address these kinds of situations:

- Present information to staff members that lets them know how a topic of discussion will affect their work.
- Ask the team to talk about how a seemingly unrelated agenda item could affect them immediately or in the near future.
- Provide staff members with detailed timelines that outline when final decisions need to be made; let them know month by month what needs to be addressed.
- Give staff members information about how upcoming issues will affect the school; help them to understand how their input may influence the final decision.
- Be honest in letting teachers know which issues they need to focus on and which issues they don't need to worry about at this point in the year.
- Provide a printed schedule of some of the major staff meeting ideas or themes for the upcoming year; let teachers know which items they should be involved in and which don't require discussion at the staff meeting level.
- Provide a list of all of the issues that may affect the school over the next few months; after discussing these issues, let staff members prioritize them in the order they will be discussed.

Inappropriate Use of Time at a Meeting

As the meeting leader, it is up to you to make sure the meeting time is used appropriately. If you call people together, you should use their combined thinking and problem-solving capacities. Don't call a meeting and engage people in a process that could be accomplished through another, less time-consuming method.

A common culprit of ineffective meetings is getting the staff together only to read a list of announcements to them. In most cases, there is a more efficient way to disseminate information than reading it to a group of people at a staff meeting. If you have trouble with people not reading and understanding announcements, then you may have an exception to this rule—but in most cases, adults can be trusted to read information that has been printed or sent to them by e-mail.

Common time wasters include the following:

- Not starting a meeting at its scheduled time
- Discussing relatively unimportant topics at length
- Asking a group for input on a decision that could be made by a leader or subgroup
- Complaining rather than problem solving
- Allowing one group to dominate the meeting agenda
- Allowing the meeting agenda to become too full; not allowing topics to be fully discussed or examined
- Waiting for team members to arrive at a meeting past the prearranged starting time

Ways to Deal With This Barrier

There may be many causes for inappropriate use of time during a staff meeting. Here are some remedies that some of our colleagues have used:

- Review meeting agendas or minutes to make sure the topics presented really need to be shared in a meeting setting.
- Examine agenda items to see whether they could be resolved more efficiently by task forces, subcommittees, decisions by the leader, etc.
- Look at agenda items to see what kind of action is needed. If they need group processing, bringing them to a group meeting is a good idea. Consider writing the type of action needed next to each agenda item to guide the group in its thinking and processing.
- Be honest in evaluating the amount of time needed to resolve agenda items; schedule fewer items than you think you can address during the time allotted for the meeting.
- Set and follow group norms for effective meetings to prevent one group from taking over the agenda; be watchful of balanced

participation in meetings and call on those who are not involved in the discussion to share their thoughts.

- Select a staff member to be the timekeeper to keep the group moving forward on its preestablished agenda.
- If you find that people cannot make it to the meeting on time, talk with them privately to see how this situation could be resolved.
- If a significant number of the participants are coming to meetings late and holding up the starting time, consider changing the start time of your meetings.
- Provide a reminder to get people to meetings on time; consider using music, announcements, or other methods to get people to the meetings.
- Examine agendas to see whether the meetings contain items and activities of substance or whether they are dull and boring; this may keep people away from the beginning of the meeting.
- Provide door prizes and other incentives to get people to the meeting on time.
- During the last five minutes of the meeting, talk with the group and evaluate your use of time during the meeting: Was the meeting productive, or did people find the meeting a waste of time?

Peer Pressure

In almost every group of staff members, there are teachers who want to control the meeting process. These people can exert pressure on the rest of the teachers that keeps them from becoming a productive group. We recently worked with a school in which the sixth-grade team controlled the staff meetings and kept them very negative. The rest of the teachers were afraid to speak up and share ideas in meetings because they knew the sixth-grade teachers would confront them about their positive actions in private. The peer pressure of this senior group kept the rest of the staff from moving forward as a school.

Ways to Deal With This Barrier

Peer pressure can be difficult to undo, but here are some strategies to consider:

- Develop the strength of positive factions in your school and diminish the influence of negative factions; reward positive behaviors with comments and support people as they work through the stages to become more positive.
- Meet with individuals from the negative group and explain what you are trying to accomplish; try to determine whether

your efforts are a threat to them and how they can agree to try the new ideas and not disrupt the process in its early stages.

- Work with a subgroup consisting of informal building leaders to address the situation; involve these team members in planning and running some parts of the staff meeting.
- Defend teachers publicly when they share good things but are attacked by negative teachers. Let the staff members know you will support people as they try new ideas.
- Talk with the whole staff and explain why you are trying to implement energizing activities, how the teachers will benefit from them, and what you expect from the teachers as your initiatives move forward. Let people know that you will work hard to support them if they run into difficulty with these energizing activities.
- Break up clusters of negative people by using random or designed grouping strategies; spreading out the negative people can diminish their influence on a staff.
- Change the room arrangement so that it is new or unfamiliar to the staff; new surroundings can work to change people's behavior, at least in the short term.
- Set and follow meeting ground rules or meeting norms. Establish ground rules yourself if you feel the group is not capable of setting its own behavioral expectations; allow the group to establish meeting norms if you think staff members are capable of doing so.

Organizational Culture

Schools can develop their own unique cultures and group behaviors to go along with that culture. Many times, people experience a lack of control or a feeling that their efforts will not move the school forward. This can become the established practice and belief among those who work at the school. Meetings then become a place where the negative feelings of the staff members come out. Because some people may never have experienced a good meeting, they may not know what one looks like or can't appreciate how good meetings can enhance their work at the school. This culture perpetuates itself in meetings and becomes a very hard habit to break.

Ways to Deal With This Barrier

Although organizational culture can take time to change, here are a few strategies to minimize this barrier:

- Let teachers know the nature of the change that will take place in your meetings; explain your rationale for wanting to improve the meetings.
- Assess the relative strength of the negative culture and what is keeping it in operation; decide how you will address the major issues experienced by the group.
- Talk about the negative aspects of the old culture of meetings; explain how the new meeting processes that you are putting in place will benefit their work and professional lives.
- Involve teachers in a discussion about how the old culture of meetings needs to change; ask them to help you develop and implement strategies to improve their meetings.
- Provide teachers with a roadmap telling them how the change in meetings will be implemented and sustained; use this roadmap to guide your improvement efforts and to remind teachers of their progress.
- Bring in an outside facilitator to help conduct meetings until a new culture is developed.
- Learn and implement self-defense strategies when you encounter negative emotions and comments associated with the change process. Some of these strategies are provided in more detail in John's book, *Effective Group Facilitation in Education* (Eller, 2004).
- Provide strategies to help staff members evaluate their growth as they implement new meeting behaviors; take a few minutes at the end of each meeting to talk about their thoughts and perceptions.

Poor Relationships Among Team Members

Some teacher groups don't get along with each other. This lack of meaningful relationships has a negative impact on the leader's ability to organize and run effective meetings. A few years ago, we had the opportunity to lead a meeting of high school staff members who were trying to make a decision about curricular offerings for the next school year. The teachers in the group had developed cliques and factions within the building. The group was unable to have a good meeting to solve its problems until we were able to get to the root of the problem and attack its poor relationship structure. This took some time, but once they began to work out their differences, they started to meet as a group and made progress toward creating a decision-making process.

Ways to Deal With This Barrier

Relationship problems can be very difficult to repair quickly, but here are some ideas that we have found to be successful in working with groups in the past:

- Hold a meeting with the "informal" leaders of the groups that are not getting along; offer to help them work out their differences.
- Meet with individuals who are not getting along; offer to help mediate their problems.
- Develop ground rules governing interactions in meetings to ensure that all parties at the meeting feel safe.
- Hold an open meeting and ask the parties in conflict to work out their differences.

Poor Relationship Between the Leader and Team Members

In some schools, there are relationship problems between the leader and the teachers. In these settings, it is almost impossible for good meetings to happen. Some of the relationship problems we have observed in our work with schools and districts include the following:

- Lack of respect for the leader by teachers in the group
- Lack of respect for teachers by the leader
- Top-down management style of leadership in which the teachers have no say in decisions in the building
- Verbal intimidation of teachers by the leader
- Lack of direction from the leader
- Situations in which the teachers feel the leader doesn't listen to their ideas
- Situations in which the teachers feel the leader doesn't care about them

Ways to Deal With This Barrier

This can be the most difficult relationship problem to address because the issue may be you or the supervisor–supervisee relationship involved. Try these ideas to gain an understanding of the problem and to begin to address the teachers' issues:

- Administer a confidential staff survey to ask for feedback about your leadership; analyze the results of the survey and set goals based on what you learn.

- Talk with informal building leaders and find out what has been causing the major problems; work with them to address the problems.
- Ask teacher-leaders to begin implementing energizing activities; once the staff is comfortable with the process of doing them, gradually begin to lead some of them yourself.
- Reflect on how you conduct staff meetings and honestly assess how your behavior affects others in the meeting.
- Gather evidence of your meeting behaviors using a video camera or tape recorder; view or listen to this evidence and note how your behaviors affect the group members.
- Hold an open meeting with staff; let them know you are interested in improving your meeting behaviors and need their help with your improvement initiatives. Ask them for verbal or written feedback on your efforts.
- Work with a colleague to assess your leadership characteristics and make adjustments based on the feedback you receive.

In these and other situations that we have observed, until the relationship problems get worked out among the teachers and the leader, it is very difficult to hold good meetings.

Past Meeting Experiences

Almost everyone can recall a time when they have attended or participated in a really bad meeting. This negative emotion can carry over to other meetings. It is important for the meeting leader to use framing techniques to send the message that this meeting will not be like those other ineffective meetings. If the teachers' negative experiences originated from previous meetings facilitated by this leader, then he or she needs to tell the group how the new meetings will be different. In addition, the leader needs to make sure that none of the problems that group members experienced in the past are repeated in future meetings.

Ways to Deal With This Barrier

Like the strategies used in the previous example, which was related to erasing the experiences of the old meeting culture, the strategies here require you to replace teachers' old thought patterns with new ideas about how meetings will be conducted in the future. Some of those strategies are illustrated in the following list:

- Have the group talk about and write down the pros and cons of their old meetings. Talk about the new methods that will replace the old structure and post these methods while disposing of the old meeting ideas that were written down.
- Work with the group to set norms for meeting operations that include effective meeting strategies and behaviors; post these norms in the regular meeting room so that all can see them and refer to them when needed.
- Form a study team to examine the effectiveness of your present meetings. Have this group share its findings and make recommendations to the whole staff at a future meeting.
- Explain to your staff why you want to change meetings and how you plan to improve them. Be fairly detailed in your description of the new meeting structure you plan to implement.
- Ask groups of teachers to think about some of their negative meeting experiences. Ask them to make a meaningful presentation illustrating these negative experiences.

Lack of Control Over Meetings

Teachers traditionally have not had much control over meeting agendas. This lack of control may lead them to disconnect from the meeting process or even to sabotage their staff meetings. Implementing energizing activities gets everyone involved during the meeting. Some leaders even have their teachers plan and conduct the energizing activities for their meetings. This practice really gets the teachers involved and engaged in the process of the meeting.

Ways to Deal With This Barrier

Here are several strategies to consider in addressing this barrier:

- Set the next meeting agenda at the present meeting while everyone is still in the room.
- Meet with a small subcommittee to design the agenda for the upcoming meeting.
- Have a suggestion box in place where people can put their ideas for future agenda items.
- Ask a small group of teachers to be responsible for conducting opening energizers at your meetings.

Poorly Planned or Implemented Agendas

Agendas that are poorly planned or even nonexistent act as a barrier to effective meetings. An agenda acts as a structural foundation for an effective meeting. Well-planned and well-paced agendas provide your teachers a chance to explore topics thoroughly and to make effective decisions. Agendas that have too many items for serious consideration make people feel rushed and don't allow them the time they need to make effective decisions. Meetings at which no agenda has been developed or shared with participants tend to wander around within a variety of topics. Both conditions contribute to people's expectations of a poor meeting.

Ways to Deal With This Barrier

Consider these ideas if you are interested in addressing this barrier:

- Work with a planning committee to set the agendas for future meetings.
- Assign time limits for specific agenda items; follow these in the meeting.
- Ask staff members to rate their priorities for topics on the agenda at the beginning of the meeting.
- Use a priority rating system to decide which agenda items need the most time in the meeting.
- Have a colleague review your agendas before they are sent to staff; ask this person to identify any items that could be handled through written announcements outside the meeting and to give you feedback on the time you have allocated for topics on the agenda.
- Review your planned agendas and compare them with what actually was accomplished at recent meetings; look for areas of variance between what was planned and what was implemented and make adjustments to future agendas based on this analysis.

Identification Techniques

Although most barriers can be easily spotted by school leaders, there are some things that leaders may be challenged to fully understand. See how this plays out in the following example:

As he was getting ready to start the meeting, Tom noticed blank looks coming from his teachers. He asked several questions of the group, but only a couple of teachers were willing to talk. Obviously, this made Tom very nervous because he was relatively new at the school. When he asked the entire group why they were not participating in the discussion, two teachers said that this was a quiet group. Tom didn't believe this and wanted to find out more.

In our work with school leaders, the situation that Tom faced is not unusual. The problem in this situation is that the teachers do not talk during their meetings; it is important for Tom to get to the bottom of why this behavior is occurring. People may be reluctant to talk about the issues that are keeping them from working together as a group. It will probably take some investigative work on Tom's part to get to the bottom of the issue.

You may be wondering, why would someone spend time trying to figure this problem out when there are so many other pressing issues to deal with? The simple answer is that, at this time, this is the most pressing issue facing this school. If team members cannot learn to work together in meetings, they are likely to have problems working together for the good of students in the school. Here are some tools to help you dig deeper and get to the bottom of the issue.

Individual Staff Interviews

A strategy that we have had much success with is conducting individual teacher interviews. You normally can set these up so that they last 15–20 minutes. In these interviews, it is crucial to ask questions that will help you put together the puzzle and find out what is causing the problems. After you have spent some time setting the tone, move into your questions and take notes; you will gain information that will be helpful to you.

In setting up these interviews, you can let the teachers know, in a memo or verbally at a staff meeting, that you would like to meet with each of them to talk about how everyone can work together to make the school a great place for teachers and students. Set up 20-minute time slots and let people sign up for a time. Try to schedule these interviews within a two-week period, if possible, so that they don't drag on too long. Let the teachers know that you are really interested in their thoughts and ideas, then sit back and learn!

Here is a template for an interview agenda that you can use or modify to meet your needs in conducting these interviews:

Template for a Problem-Solving Interview Agenda

Keep in mind that you are asking your teachers to talk about something that might be hard for them to discuss: the dysfunctional behavior of their colleagues. Some will be more willing to share their thoughts than others. Be patient and take the information they are willing to share with you. If you push too hard, you may make some of them less willing to talk. You have to reassure them that the information is for you and will not be used to "get" anyone on the staff.

Consider these steps when conducting the interviews:

- Set a professional tone at the beginning of the meeting.

    Example: "Thank you for making the time to meet with me today. I'd like to spend the next 15–20 minutes talking with you about ways that we can improve our school."

- Pose a broad question that asks the teacher to talk about his or her general perceptions of the school.

    Example: "In general, how do you think our school is doing in helping students to learn and grow?"

- Ask a more focused question to help the teacher think about some of the specific ways the school is effective or could be improved.

    Example: "Specifically, when do you think we do a good job working together as a staff, and what areas do you see that we need to improve?"

- Ask a specific question about the teacher's perceptions of staff meetings.

    Example: "What are your thoughts about how our staff meetings are conducted? What seems to go well, and what seems to not go very well?"

- Ask a specific question about what the teacher thinks is causing the staff meeting problems.

    Example: "From your perspective, what do you think is causing the majority of the problems at our staff meetings?"

- Ask the teacher to share how he or she thinks the situation could be improved.

    Example: "What do you think we need to do to begin to solve the issues you mentioned?"

- Thank the teacher for his or her thoughts and for meeting with you.

    Example: "Thank you for taking the time to meet with me and for sharing your perspectives on our school."

Teacher Questionnaires

Another tool that can give you information about the barriers behind the visible staff meeting problems you encounter is the confidential questionnaire. Many school leaders administer periodic questionnaires to their teachers to learn their perceptions of a variety of school issues. A questionnaire can be fairly simple, consisting of a few questions on a single page. Traditionally, school leaders have typed their questions on paper, handed out the questionnaires, and placed a box in the office or some other prominent location for depositing the completed forms. There are now Web-based instruments that can be e-mailed to teachers and completed online. These instruments allow teachers to complete the questionnaire confidentially and automatically tabulate the results. One that we have found to be particularly easy to use is called Survey Monkey. This site even has a free trial option. It can be found at www.surveymonkey.com.

Here we offer two sample questionnaires.

ABC School Questionnaire

Thank you for taking the time to complete this questionnaire. I will keep your responses confidential but will use the information to improve our school and our staff meeting processes.

Use a scale from 1 to 4. A rating of 1 is the lowest possible score and a rating of 4 is the highest possible score.

1. Rate our school's ability to work with and help students. _____

2. Rate our school's ability to provide a stimulating professional atmosphere for teachers. _____

3. Rate the effectiveness of our staff meetings. _____

4. What do you think are our biggest challenges to good staff meetings?

   _____

5. How can our staff meetings be improved?

   _____

XYZ Questionnaire

Thank you for taking the time to complete this questionnaire. I will keep your responses confidential but will use the information to improve our school and our staff meeting processes.

1. In general, how does the present organization of our staff meetings help you as a teacher?

2. What barriers or problems are present in our staff meetings that get in the way of our effectiveness?

3. How can we improve our staff meetings?

4. What are you willing to do to improve our staff meetings?

Summary and Next Steps

In this chapter, we examined the most common barriers to meeting effectiveness, learned ways to identify them and their root causes, and devised ways to help groups work through them. In addition to these ideas, we also explored how to engage your staff in helping to eliminate barriers and make staff meetings more productive and energizing to attend.

Obviously, as the meeting leader, you have the primary responsibility for identifying and eliminating these barriers, but a key tactic that many effective meeting leaders have used is to get the participants involved and engaged in solving their own problems. By being a part of the solution rather than waiting for you to fix the problem, your staff members will be more invested in positively resolving the situation. As a meeting leader, if you can get your staff more involved, they will develop ownership—the kind of ownership you will need to move your staff forward toward greater effectiveness.

As you finish this chapter, take a few minutes to reflect on the following questions:

- What barriers are holding back my meetings, and what is my plan for dealing with them?
- Which key staff members do I need to work with to identify and attack the problems we have at our meetings?
- What strategies and techniques can I begin to use immediately to improve the effectiveness of my meetings?

- How will I measure my progress in removing barriers and helping my team members to work together in a productive manner?

Use the information you have learned here to make your meetings powerful and energizing experiences for all of your staff. In the end, they win and you win with a more motivated and engaged staff!

Energized staff meetings have great starts. In Chapter 3, "Great Beginnings," we will share strategies to get your next meeting off to a great start. This is a first and crucial step in improving the quality and functioning of your meetings. We know you will find many practical ideas and strategies that you can implement immediately in almost any existing meeting structure.

3

Great Beginnings

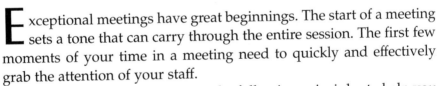

What we call results are beginnings.

—Ralph Waldo Emerson

Exceptional meetings have great beginnings. The start of a meeting sets a tone that can carry through the entire session. The first few moments of your time in a meeting need to quickly and effectively grab the attention of your staff.

In this chapter, you will learn the following principles to help you jump-start your meetings:

- Attention grabbers that get everyone involved right at the start of a meeting
- Ways to frame and connect with the positive emotions of staff
- Specific activities to help staff unload the baggage that has built up during the day and to reframe their emotions so that they are ready to participate
- Methods to recharge and energize your staff
- Strategies to put staff members in a creative and problem-solving mind-set
- Ideas to make your meetings more fun and engaging
- Ways to assess the results of your energizing efforts

The Importance of the Start

Humans are extremely emotional beings; we use our emotions to shape our behaviors. Tied closely to emotions is the principle of attention grabbing. You see these principles in play all around you as you go about your daily life. Television commercials strive to get our attention and play to our emotions to get us to make purchasing decisions. Movies use tightly choreographed scenes and music to put us in a certain mood as we watch a story unfold. Public speakers may share a touching story with us at the beginning of a speech to grab our attention and shape our emotions. In staff meetings, emotions and attention play important roles in setting the tone for effectiveness. Here are some principles to keep in mind—think about their importance in your staff meetings:

Emotional and Attention-Getting Needs

- ✓ In many schools, staff meetings are held at the end of the day. During the day, many events may have influenced the emotions of staff members. Teachers may have had negative encounters with parents, conflicts with students, or even disagreements with colleagues. All of these negative emotional experiences can affect your meeting unless you reframe the teachers' thinking.
- ✓ Staff may have settled into typical meeting behaviors. These may include talking with others while the meeting is in progress, grading papers during the meeting, not participating in staff discussions, etc. Grabbing their attention and setting an emotional tone can help to avoid these behaviors.
- ✓ As the leader, you may have developed patterns for how you operate meetings. It is easy to fall into a rut that promotes dull meetings, such as reading information to staff, plowing through an agenda, or neglecting to find out what others think about a situation.
- ✓ In some staffs, senior members can exert control over younger staff by putting pressure on them not to participate in discussions. Implementing activities that all staff members are asked to participate in can give new staff a voice in the decision-making process.
- ✓ Many times, our staff members may have trouble seeing new solutions to the problems they face. Implementing attention-getting activities can help them break their old patterns of thinking and look at problems from different perspectives.
- ✓ In some schools, the focus on work and school improvement has taken some of the fun out of teaching and leading. Emotional and attention-getting meeting starters can help staff to blow off steam and have fun at the work site.

Setting the Stage With Music

Music can be a powerful way to energize people because of the way it quickly connects with deep emotions. If you stop and listen carefully, you'll find there is music present in almost every part of our modern lives. In many cases, this music influences our emotions and decisions. We will explore how you can use this powerful ally to help you set and keep a positive tone in your meetings. First, we will look at the use of music to start meetings. As you think about using music to start your meetings, consider following a template to help you use music strategically to grab attention and set a positive tone for your meetings.

All of these questions can help you decide just how you might use music to start a meeting. In thinking about using music at the start of the meeting, some reflection and planning will be very helpful to you. Not only will you need to think about the emotional tone you would like to set at the beginning of the meeting, you also will have to think about what types of music might motivate your group and how teachers might react to your use of music at the beginning of a meeting. Obviously, it is important to keep in mind the purpose of using music in the first place—to grab attention and to set the proper emotional tone for your group. Consider the following examples and how the meeting leaders used music to build positive emotions with the staff.

Jim was getting ready to start his staff meeting. During the last few months, he had noticed that people looked really tired at the start of his staff meetings. He knew he needed to do something to start his meetings in a more positive manner. He decided to play the theme from the movie *Rocky* to start his meeting. As teachers came into the meeting, they heard the song playing in the background. Jim observed people's reactions. Some began to smile, and others started to move with the music. As the song played on, Jim noticed that people seemed to be energized. When the song was over, he enthusiastically welcomed people to the meeting and asked them how they felt. He received several comments about the increased energy level they had experienced. A couple of staff members also commented that they wanted to go out and rent the movie *Rocky* for the evening.

Nora felt that her staff members seemed nervous and anxious at the start of her staff meetings. The school she leads is a very high-energy place where students demand a lot of attention. This carried over to the staff meetings, where people wanted to move quickly and make rash decisions. She knew that she needed to help people to relax and shed anxiety. She decided to play soft, engaging music at the start of her meeting while people were arriving and milling around. She chose to play

"Somewhere Out There" from *An American Tale* and "Hero" by Mariah Carey. The music seemed to calm people down and help them settle in and relax. She asked her staff how they liked the music. Most of them responded that it was soothing. She found that staff members were able to sit down and think through decisions more carefully as a result of the emotional tone she had set with her two musical selections.

In both of these examples, the leaders of the meetings thought carefully about the proper emotional tone that needed to be set for the staff. They used the music to grab the attention of the staff members. Each leader was faced with a challenge but found an appropriate song to meet his or her group's needs. In the two examples, the leaders also talked with staff about their perceptions of the music. This is a key point because leaders need to find out how different types of music affect their staff. At times, leaders may find that certain types of songs don't resonate with their teachers. In those instances, they may put those types of music on the back burner. At times, leaders wonder what songs seem to work best to start meetings with teachers. There is no magic song that meets the needs of every group or situation. The success of the music depends on the needs of the group. We have found that the same song may cause a slightly different reaction when used in a slightly different situation. Use your intuition and knowledge of the group to help you select songs to energize your staff meetings. See page 40 for a list of some of the songs we have used with groups to grab their attention and to set a positive tone at the beginning of meetings.

Other Uses for Music at the Start of Meetings

In addition to setting a tone, there are other activities in which music can help to improve your staff meetings.

- Name That Tune: This is a spin-off of the show of the same name. As a warm-up for the meeting, teachers can be organized into small teams of three or four. A short part of a song is played, and they are asked to name the tune or some other significant aspect of the song. At the end of several rounds, the team with the most points is declared the winner.
- Memories: This strategy is designed to set a positive emotional feeling among teachers. Several songs that have a common familiarity are played for the entire group. Teachers are asked to identify a positive experience they have had or associate

Music Planning Template	
Questions to Consider	**Specific Responses for the Group**
What emotions have teachers built up during the day that need to released at the start of a meeting?	
What kind of tone am I looking to set in the meeting?	
What kinds of music do people in my group seem to like?	
What is the reaction of group members when they hear music?	
What is the age group of those attending the meeting? What type of music would resonate with these participants?	
What will help to energize me as I prepare to lead the meeting?	
What messages will the lyrics of the songs I choose subconsciously send to my participants? How can I use the songs to build a culture of collaboration?	

Music to Use During Staff Meetings

Song Title	Artist	Source	Situations for Use
"Circle of Life," "Can You Feel the Love Tonight?"	Elton John	Soundtrack from *The Lion King*	To set a collaborative tone
"Tapestry of Nations"	London Symphony	Disney's *Millennium Celebration Album*	To motivate a group
"(I've Had) The Time of My Life"	Bill Medley and Jennifer Warnes	Soundtrack from *Dirty Dancing*	At the end of a meeting segment
"Time Passages"	Al Stewart	*Greatest Hits*	To calm a group
"Top of the World"	The Carpenters	*Greatest Hits*	To set a positive tone
"Stayin' Alive"	Bee Gees	Soundtrack from *Saturday Night Fever*	To fire up and motivate a group
"Roll on Down the Highway," "Takin' Care of Business"	Bachman-Turner Overdrive	*Greatest Hits*	To fire up or motivate a group
"You're the One That I Want"	John Travolta and Olivia Newton-John	Soundtrack from *Grease*	To lighten up the atmosphere
"Gonna Fly Now"		Rocky I soundtrack	Fire up a group, call them to a meeting
"Eye of the Tiger"	Survivor	Soundtrack from *Rocky III*	To fire up a group
"Yesterday Once More"	The Carpenters	*Yesterday Once More* (Greatest Hits)	To calm a group
"A Hard Day's Night," "I Want to Hold Your Hand"	The Beatles	*The Beatles 1*	To fire up a group
"Somewhere Out There"	James Ingram and Linda Ronstadt	*Greatest Hits: Power of Great Music*	To set a positive tone
"Yah Mo B There"	James Ingram and Michael McDonald	*Greatest Hits: Power of Great Music*	To fire up a group
"Heard It in a Love Song"	The Marshall Tucker Band	*The Marshall Tucker Band*	To set an energizing tone
"Shamanic Dream"	Anugama-Werner Hagen	*Spiritual Environment* (Nightingale Records)	To provide background music for working groups, relaxation
"Say You, Say Me"	Lionel Richie	*Back to Front* (Greatest Hits)	To set a tone of anticipation
"Morning Has Broken"	Cat Stevens	*Greatest Hits*	To relax a group
"That's the Way It Is"	Celine Dion	*All the Way: A Decade of Song*	To set an energetic tone
"Rhythm Is Gonna Get You"	Gloria Estefan	*Greatest Hits*	To set an energetic tone

with the song. After a few minutes, they are asked to share their stories in small groups. This strategy helps to reshape their emotions and gets teachers to talk with each other at the beginning of the meeting.

- This Reminds Me: This strategy is a variation of the memories activity. As each song is played, teachers are asked to identify a student from their classroom whom the song reminds them of. The reminder could be in relation to the lyrics, the tune, the tempo of the music, or whatever criteria are used by the teachers. Teachers are asked to share their associations in small groups. At the end of the activity, they are asked to talk about what they learned as a result of their thinking.

Meeting Starters

Starting a meeting in the proper manner helps to set the tone you need for productive thinking and problem solving to occur. It is especially important when you want to energize your staff meetings. Here are some ideas that can be used at the beginning of a meeting to set the tone and to begin the process of energizing your staff meetings.

Trivia Questions

Trivia questions can help to set a positive tone and make the beginning of your meeting attractive for your teachers. Questions are placed on a board or on a large tablet where they can be seen as people enter the meeting room. This activity is conducted in teams of three to four people. Specific directions for the group activity are written above the questions. As teachers enter the meeting, they are asked to read the directions and to answer as many questions as possible in the specified period of time. The team with the most correct answers at the end of the specified time is declared the winner. In addition to changing the meeting dynamics, this activity also challenges the thinking and problem-solving skills of teachers and gets their creative juices flowing. Building up the thinking and problem-solving skills of teachers is essential to help them solve more complex problems in other situations that the staff may face in the future. This activity gives them some light practice in the skill. Here are some ideas for trivia themes that may interest your staff:

- Questions relating to facts about the building or the school neighborhood, such as the age of the building or demographics: These facts and questions can be generated by veteran staff, parent volunteers, or other community experts.

- Questions relating to events that have happened at the school or to students during the school year: These questions could include topics such as student council activities, playground stories, assembly topics, the amount of food collected during the most recent food drive, the number of bands at the school talent show, information from a recent staff development presentation, or other topics of interest to the staff or school-related events that may hold meaning for the teachers. Teams of teachers could generate the questions related to school events.
- Questions relating to personal or professional information about staff members: These questions could include items such as staff who have recently completed master's degrees, teachers who are grandparents and the names of their grandchildren, staff working on home-remodeling projects, teachers who have served in the most buildings during their careers, and other professional or personal information.
- Questions from commercially prepared games related to popular topics such as movies, politics, literature, and other cultural information: The cards supplied with these games can be drawn and used to generate all kinds of trivia questions.

There are many ways to implement a trivia experience at the beginning of a meeting. Here are a few variations you may consider trying with your staff:

- Individual Trivia: Teachers answer trivia questions individually from a list of questions posted on chart paper.
- Card Trivia: Teachers are given a card when they enter the meeting. The card contains a set of trivia questions for each teacher to complete. A set amount of time is provided and the person with the most correct answers is declared the winner.
- Interdependent Trivia: In this game, a set of trivia questions is provided to the teachers, but their job is to work together to answer as many trivia questions correctly as possible. Team members may use any configuration to work together to solve the trivia questions: They can meet in pairs, triplets, or some other configuration. Each team needs to decide which configuration will allow them to answer the questions as quickly and accurately as possible. The meeting leader may have the group work together for pride or offer prizes for solving a set number of questions.

- Question Generation: In this variation, the team leader lists a series of answers and teams work to generate questions that correspond to the answers. The answers provided need to be subtle and not easily connected to the questions so that the activity is moderately challenging to the participants. This variation works with individuals or groups.
- Stump Your Opponent: In this trivia competition, the staff is divided into two teams. The teams take turns generating trivia questions that they administer to the opposing team. Their goal is to generate questions that will stump the other team. The teams are restricted to generating trivia questions within a set category. For example, the meeting leader might name the general category of school history. Both teams would work to generate trivia questions within the category of school history. Once the questions are generated, the teams take turns administering them to each other. In the end, the team that answers the most trivia questions correctly wins the exercise.

When using trivia activities to start staff meetings, it is important to keep several things in mind. A clear plan for starting the meeting is essential. Let staff members know why you are using the strategy to start the meeting. The strategy should be implemented in a quick and efficient manner to keep teachers focused and productive. If the activity goes on too long, teachers will feel it is a waste of time. In most cases, the activity should be wrapped up in three to five minutes. Be sure to debrief the activity at the end by asking teachers to reflect on what was learned as a result of the experience. The debriefing should be related mainly to what teachers learned about their work as a staff rather than the trivial knowledge that was learned as a result of the activity.

Good News

Another opener that helps to set a positive tone and encourage teachers to be engaged in the meeting is an activity called Good News. This idea is grounded in the generalization that if people are involved in positive discussion at the start of a meeting, the positive feeling will carry over to the rest of the meeting. The initial activity or discussion frames their mind-set for the topics that follow.

In the Good News opener, the meeting leader asks participants to share a bit of good news with the entire group. The news could be personal or professional but usually is brief in nature. In a group of 30 teachers, it is normal to share five to six pieces of good news during the opening of a meeting. At first, teachers may be reluctant to share, but once the ice is broken, the sharing will be easier. To help teachers through the initial discomfort related to sharing good news, there are several points to keep in mind:

- Consider asking a few teachers in advance to be ready to share a good news idea at your next faculty meeting. When you introduce the idea to the group and two or three teachers share good news right away, it helps to build the confidence of the others to share. After the staff gets accustomed to the idea of sharing good news, teachers will be more open in their sharing; you won't need to "prime the pump."
- During the meeting at which you introduce the concept, be sure to explain how the activity will work and why you are using it with the staff. If teachers know why they are engaging in an activity, they will be able to relate to it better than if it appears to come out of nowhere.
- At the end of the good news portion of the meeting, take a minute to ask teachers what they learned from the activity and their perceptions of it. This helps them move to a deeper level of understanding and reflection about their own learning.
- Ask teachers to think about how this activity might be used in the classroom with students. This helps them to move to a deeper level of reflection and understanding of the strategy, and it gives them activities they can consider using in their classrooms. Teachers appreciate additional strategies and ideas to make their classrooms more engaging. We have had teachers talk about these kinds of strategies in meetings and then, because of their interest, implement them the next day in school. Teachers like to see their leaders using effective teaching strategies in their work.
- Build in Good News as an agenda item with its own time and place on the agenda. If you don't, it could be left out or neglected. For most groups, the Good News activity takes place at the beginning of a meeting. This helps to start off the meeting positively and gets people involved right away.
- As group members bring up positive examples and at the end of the Good News session, be sure to reinforce them for their efforts. Make sure you are sincere in your praise so that they will continue to participate in Good News sessions in the future.

- When you first introduce the idea of sharing good news, there may be some reluctance on the part of staff to talk in front of the group. This could cause several moments of silence. As the person who is standing in front of the group waiting for people to share, you may feel uncomfortable and want to move on too quickly. Resist this impulse and allow teachers the wait time they need to come forth with their ideas. This could be a difficult task for some people. If much time passes and people still haven't shared an idea, consider rephrasing the request, providing prompts, or focusing your request to someone in the group you know will be able to respond. Once you have "primed the pump," more people should share ideas.

- If you know your group may have difficulty sharing good news, provide them with a focus prompt at the beginning of the activity. Focus prompts that have local meaning and context work best for meeting leaders, but here are some that we have used that have helped people to get focused and share their thoughts during Good News sessions:

    Share something good that has happened to you since our last time together.

    What ideas have you thought about in relation to our task since our last meeting?

    Share something that has been good news to you since we last met.

    Talk about a positive that you have experienced as a result of being on this team.

    Find a partner and talk about something good that happened to you this week.

    Think about a situation where you have recently encountered something that was potentially negative, but through your efforts, it became positive.

    Share an example of someone you know who helps to make your day when you see them.

Besides setting a tone and encouraging people to participate in a meeting, Good News has other benefits for your staff. Here are a few of those benefits:

- The strategy allows teachers to get to know more personal and professional information about each other. When colleagues have a deeper understanding of each other, they are able to work together better than when they have just a surface relationship.

- Using Good News breaks the old meeting patterns and lets teachers approach the agenda topics with a fresh look.
- In advanced stages of the Good News process, staff members begin to share positive examples of what they have experienced in working with other staff members. It is important that they recognize each other and their efforts. This provides another channel for feedback, which is important to professionals. It also shows you, the meeting leader, that they are beginning to develop collegial relationships. These relationships are important to the health of the school.
- Teachers will eventually begin to share student- and parent-related good news as they become more comfortable with the activity. This is important because it helps teachers to see the positive side of their clients and counteracts the negative talk that can invade a staff meeting.
- Using the Good News strategy allows you to model effective instructional practices and puts you in a good light with your staff members. It is easier for them to implement good instruction in their classrooms once they see you modeling ideas for them.

There are many different ways to implement the idea of having staff members share their good news with others. Here are a few that we have used in recent staff meetings.

- Department Reporting: In this strategy, the staff is divided into grade-level or departmental groups. Each group is asked to share a piece of good news or a happening that occurred in the department or grade level during the past month. The meeting opens with each group briefly sharing its item with the whole faculty.
- Good News Turns: This variation is similar to the Department Reporting strategy. Teachers are organized into grade levels or departments, but the reporting occurs slightly differently. In this strategy, a department or grade level is assigned to do the good news section at a meeting. During its assigned meeting time, the grade level or department shares five or six pieces of good news.
- Good News For All: Some meeting leaders have used this idea to help staff members learn how to share good news ideas. At

the beginning of the meeting, all teachers are asked to stand. They are told to form pairs with people on the staff whom they normally have little interaction with on a day-to-day basis. Each pair is given one to two minutes to share a good news announcement. At the end of the designated time, the meeting leader calls the group to attention and asks individuals to share a good news item they heard while meeting with their partner. This strategy can help open people up and get the positive contributions of individuals out to the larger staff. It can help some of those teachers who are a little shy to share their own ideas. Some people don't like to share their own thoughts but will share what they hear another person talk about. This variation gets everyone participating at the beginning of a meeting because they are talking in pairs. It helps to get positive ideas out on the table and gives staff members a chance to learn more about each other.

- Good News Notes: Some groups may need a more personal strategy to help them learn how to do the good news opener. They may do well with this idea. All teachers are given a slip of paper the day before a staff meeting that has a prompt on it asking them to write down something good that happened to them lately, either personally or professionally. They are instructed to bring this slip of paper to the meeting. All of the slips are shuffled and given out to the staff members randomly. Because each staff member gets someone else's good news slip, their job is to read it, find the author, and have a discussion about their good news item. Because everyone has a slip and is working to find a way to get together with the authors all at once, the activity may get a little chaotic. You can either let the chaos happen briefly, or you could structure the activity to keep it more controlled. In structuring the activity, you might consider dividing the staff members into two groups, then putting the good news slips in the drawing box. You could designate one half of the staff members as Group A and the other half as Group B. All of the slips for the teachers from the B group could be placed in a box and drawn by the A group members. Once these members have been interviewed, the process could be reversed. This type of organizational structure could be used to make sure the activity flows smoothly. The purpose of the good news notes strategy is to give teachers a way to interact with each other as they learn more about each other and set a positive meeting tone.

Human Bingo

This is a highly engaging and energizing activity for teachers and others whom you may be working with in a meeting setting. It not only gets people up and moving around the room, it also engages them in a dialogue about each other. The activity works like this:

- At the start of the meeting, each person is given a card that is laid out like a bingo card (see illustration).
- Within each square of the bingo card, there is a question or statement that describes a person on the team. All of the cards ask for identical information from participants. Some examples could include the following:

    Find the person in the room who has three grandchildren.

    Locate someone who attended an Ivy League college.

    Identify the person who drove the most miles on their last summer vacation.

    Find people who are doing a home-remodeling project.

    Find the person who has eaten the most unusual food.

    Identify the teacher who has been in the profession the longest.

    Locate someone who has taught in at least three buildings.

- Once all staff members have a card, they are asked to find people who fit into the categories on the card.
- When a person is found who satisfies the category listed in the square on the card, his or her name is written in the square and an X is placed in the square. That square is considered filled.
- Like the game of bingo, people try to fill their cards in rows, diagonals, or other preestablished patterns.
- The first person who fills the bingo card calls out "Bingo!" and wins the activity.

The basic Human Bingo game can be implemented in a variety of ways depending on how much time is available and the amount of interaction that is desired by the meeting leader. Here are a few variations you may consider using with your staff members:

- Team Bingo: The teachers are divided into small teams of three to five. They work as a team to fill the bingo card, but they must

Human Bingo

B	I	N	G	O
Find a staff member who has more than four grandchildren.	Identify someone on our staff who has worked overseas.	Locate a teacher who can answer this question: Who was the first principal of our school?	Find a teacher on our staff who is enrolled in a graduate program.	Look around and locate the person who has the largest junk collection.
Who on our staff has built a new home?	Which staff member was born the farthest distance from our school?	Who has taught in the most buildings?	Which staff member has the most children?	Locate a staff member who has an interesting summer job.
Which staff member has traveled the most outside the United States?	Who has the taught the most students of former students in their classroom?	Free Space	Find someone with an unusual hobby.	Find someone with a funny student-related story.
Find someone with a warm-hearted student-related story.	Who on our staff has eaten the most unusual food?	Which staff members were born closest to this school?	Who drove the longest on their last summer vacation?	Find the staff member who has met the most famous person.
Find the staff member who has had the most teaching assignments over the years.	Who has experienced the most unusual vacation?	Find someone who has an unusual zoo story.	Identify the staff member with the most pets.	Locate the person who has been in or on the tallest building or landform.

find people who are not members of their team to fill the various categories on the card. This can be challenging for groups to work through the process of moving around and talking with other team members.

- Charade Bingo: In this variation, teachers are asked to work as teams or individuals to find people to fill their bingo card. The person they find to satisfy a category must communicate his or her answer using only nonverbal means of communication. For example, if one of the categories relates to the distance traveled from home, the person must use gestures, fingers, etc., to describe the distance. In another example, for the category of most unusual food eaten, the person describing the food must use only nonverbal means in the description. As you can see, this variation has the potential to take people out of their comfort zones, but it also can create a great tone and open up thinking for people. Because this variation takes longer to develop, it may be a good idea to reduce the number of squares that need to be filled.

- Exaggeration Bingo: Teachers can be great storytellers, and this variation of the game provides them with the opportunity to practice this skill. A similar bingo matrix is used, but in this variation, the person responding to the square must fit the basic category but must add some kind of exaggeration to his or her story. The person listening to the story must decide what the exaggeration is and name it. If their guess is correct, they get to fill the square; if not, they don't. After everyone has had an opportunity to work on filling their squares, the meeting leader asks group members to share the greatest exaggerations they heard as they completed the task. This provides fun and a chance to get to know something about others as teachers work to complete the task and share their responses.

The game of Human Bingo can be a fun way to set a positive tone and encourage teachers to participate at the beginning of a meeting. There are a few considerations that need to be kept in mind as the strategy is implemented at a staff meeting.

- Be careful in generating and selecting categories that will be used in the human bingo game. Be sure to be sensitive to people's privacy and personal feelings.
- Make sure that the activity takes no longer than 8–10 minutes from beginning to end. If the activity goes a long time, it will get boring and busy staff members will see it as a waste of time.
- Be sure to share why you are doing this activity with your teachers. It helps them to understand why time has been diverted from other agenda topics to this activity.
- At the end of the activity, hold a short session during which you ask the teachers to debrief. Ask them to share what they learned as a result of the activity and how they see it benefiting their working relationships.
- Be sure to engage teachers in a discussion about how this activity could be adapted for use with students. Have them talk through the strengths and limitations of the activity for classroom use.
- Use your discussion points as a transition to the remaining agenda items for the meeting. Point out how this activity could

help staff members to better address the decisions they will face as a staff.

Problem-Solving Activities

Teachers like to be involved in generating ideas to solve common problems within the school. This natural interest in giving advice or suggestions for resolving problems can be used to set a positive tone, increase the energy level of the group, and develop problem-solving strategies.

Here is a process for conducting problem-solving starter activities with a group of teachers:

- Divide the teachers into random groups; try to combine people with others whom they normally have minimal opportunity to interact with on a regular basis.
- Generate three to four generic problems or case studies for the teams to examine. Try to find topics that could be related to real situations the school might face, but be careful that the situations don't hit too close to home. Keep the initial problems fairly simple and straightforward. Use real or realistic situations, but stay away from problems the school currently faces. If the topics are too closely related to what the teachers are experiencing in their own professional lives, it will be hard for them to design an objective solution.
- When people arrive, divide them into their groups and give them the specific directions for the activity. Try to restrict the time devoted to the activity to seven to nine minutes total.
- At the end of the work time together, ask each group to share its assessment of the situation; discuss the total learning of the group.

Here is an example of an activity recently used by a leader, Chang, to energize a group during a meeting:

Welcome to our regular staff meeting. Today, I want to engage you in an exercise to help change what we normally do at our meetings. I am asking you to work together as a team to briefly examine and share some suggestions for a set of scenarios. I am asking you to do this to help us prepare for future times when we will be working together to solve some of the problems that we are facing as a team. I have divided you into some work teams and written your situation on paper. You will have five minutes to complete the task.

Sample Task Sheet Teacher Ethics

Please read through the following situation. Within your team, talk about the situation and your ideas to help the school resolve the issue.

Situation

At the most recent parent–teacher conferences, several of the staff reported that parents were concerned that their children had not done well in math during the semester. These parents were also upset that the school had sent out a note letting parents know that they could hire the math teachers in the school to tutor their children. During the conferences, the parents said they were concerned about being asked to pay extra for tutoring when their children had not learned the prescribed curriculum.

Respond to these questions as you discuss the school-related implications of this dilemma:

What major issues need to be addressed here?
What are the valid issues from the parents' perspective?
What are the valid issues from the teachers' perspective?
How do you think the problem could be resolved?

Problem-solving activities may not work well for all teacher groups. It is important for you to examine other ways to implement the strategy to give the teachers the experience but change the way it is delivered. Here are some ideas to vary the use of problem-solving activities at the beginning of a meeting:

- Multiple-Perspective Problem Solving: In this variation, each group is given the same problem but is asked to generate ideas for its solution from a unique perspective they have been assigned. For example, some groups might generate ideas from the parent's perspective, another might address the problem from the perspective of the community, and a third group might be asked to share suggestions from the student's perspective. This variation not only asks teachers to examine a problem for ideas but also helps them to look at it from another view.
- Building on Our Solutions: This problem-solving activity involves teams of teachers who have been given problem-solving exercises that have more that one step. At each step of the problem, the team faces an either/or choice. Once the group has made its choice, it passes the problem to the next group, which needs to pick up of the situation and look at it from the

step or stage at which the previous group left off. For example, if a group was given a scenario that involved dealing with a problem related to parent–teacher conferences, their first choice might be whether to make the decision as a staff or to form an advisory committee comprising teachers and parents. If the first group chose to form an advisory committee, when they passed on the task to the next group, that next group would have to analyze the problem but could only consider the strategy of using an advisory committee in their problem-resolution process. The variation helps groups to work with problems in a constricted kind of way. In the end, the activity can be debriefed by asking each team to share its rationale for its choices in solving the problem.

To get the most from your use of problem-solving activities, be sure to keep the following considerations in mind:

- Problem-solving activities are not for every group. Think through your group's possible reaction to the strategy before introducing the concept to them.
- Make sure that the problems the group has been given are open ended in nature but are also straightforward in their approach. If there is an obvious answer, the group will experience no problem solving; if the problem is too complex and convoluted, the group members engaged in solving it will get confused and frustrated. Balance is the key to the group's success with the task.
- Stay within the time limits set at the beginning of the activity (usually about 8–10 minutes). If the activity drags on too long, the group will quickly lose interest.
- Be sure to ask questions of teachers at the end of the activity to debrief the experience. Also, make sure that they are asked to discuss how this activity could be used in classrooms with students. This will give teachers the opportunity to apply their learning in their professional practice.
- Use the strategy on a periodic basis. If it is used too often, people may get tired of it.

Synectics

The strategy of using synectics to start a meeting, set a positive, energizing tone, and encourage teachers to be active participants can be very helpful for meeting leaders looking to energize their meetings. A synectic activity involves the use of a picture, a cartoon, an example, or a story that helps to promote out-of-the-box thinking on the part of meeting participants. The meeting leader presents the object, drawing, cartoon, story, or other object to the group members and asks them to draw a comparison between it and some other idea, situation, or object. People have fun thinking about the seemingly off-task comparisons but also grow in their ability to perform analysis. Synectics can be energizing because they allow people to think and interact right at the beginning of a meeting. The list outlines the typical steps that a meeting leader would engage in while working with a group on a synectic-related activity:

- Select an object, cartoon, picture, story, or example to be presented to a group.
- Present the selected object to a group of people at the opening of the meeting; ask them to look at the object and think about how this object is like another idea, concept, problem, situation, or scenario that the leader would like the staff members to consider.
- Ask team members to work in pairs and generate responses to the task assigned to the team members.
- Allow time for all of the pair groups to share their ideas.
- Examine each item, idea, or concept and identify the particular core attribute of each
- Compare each unique list, searching for common points or shared attributes; if there are none, have the team draw some connection between the items being compared
- Put together a new idea or category that links the common attributes

During a recent staff meeting, Linda wanted her teachers to be energized at the beginning but also learn how to think more critically. She decided to make a transparency of a cartoon she had recently seen in the newspaper and show it to her staff members at the beginning of the meeting. After she showed them the cartoon and read the caption, there was some light laughter. She said, "I want you to work in pairs and have a two- to three-minute discussion about how this cartoon is like the situation we have been facing during our recent construction project." The teachers talked in pairs and generated several creative ideas of how the cartoon related to some of the problems that they had experienced during the construction project. Linda noticed that her staff members seemed more relaxed and engaged than they had in past meetings. She took a few extra minutes and asked the teachers to talk about the activity and how it helped them. She then asked them to think about how it might be adapted for use with students in classrooms. They were able to generate several ways the idea of synectics might help students to become better thinkers as a result of the activity.

In another setting, Carlos noticed that his teachers always seemed drained at the end of the day. He went down to the gym and found a small piece of gymnastic equipment. He brought it to the staff meeting and used it to start his meeting. He held up the equipment, explained what it was, and asked the teachers to consider how it was like the experience they recently had during parent–teacher conferences. In this group, Carlos had people share their initial thoughts with the entire group. He was able to listen as they shared a lot of interesting ideas. One teacher said, "The piece is a little bent, just like I felt after spending so much time talking to people." Another commented, "It is part of a greater whole, like my relationship with my parents." Many teachers found the synectic activity to be fun and engaging, and Carlos used it periodically to energize and engage his teachers.

One of the key parts of a synectic exercise is the prompt that introduces the activity and engages the thinking of the teachers, that is, the starter stem. Many people have asked how synectic activities are started. Here are some examples of starter comments that can be used in setting up synectic activities:

- How is this cartoon like the work we have to do on data analysis?
- What is similar between this chair and the difficulties we face in making the conferencing decision?
- What did you notice in my story of Jim and his victory that we could use as we move forward on our project?
- How is our recent parent–teacher organization meeting like this notebook?
- How is this picture like the emotions we face in making this decision?
- How does the person in the story I shared with you illustrate a difficulty that we face?
- What are three common characteristics that you noticed between the situation in the picture and what we face as a staff this year?

Synectics can be a powerful and effective tool to help energize staff members and shape their emotions during a meeting. There are some points of consideration that are important to the success of the use of synectics in meetings.

- Because there is no natural connection between the two ideas or objects being compared, allow people to work through their inhibitions in thinking about the concepts. When you first introduce the activity, you may get blank stares, but after a few seconds, people will warm up to the idea and participate.
- In selecting synectic source objects to be used for comparison, be careful not to pick objects for which the connection is very obvious. If the teachers are not required to think, the activity will be seen as a waste of their time.
- Accept any ideas that the teachers give you about the relationship between the comparison objects or ideas. If someone comes up with some idea that you didn't consider, that is good news.
- As people share their ideas, reinforce them for their efforts, but don't get "gushy" over the ideas they are suggesting. If you praise the first ideas that are shared too much, it will cause others to withhold their thoughts because they will think that their ideas are not worth a compliment.
- At the end of the exercise, explain the purpose of doing the synectic activity with the group. Have teachers generate ideas for its use in the classroom and talk about what they learned as a result of doing the activity in the meeting.

The term "synectics" was taken from *Pathways to Understanding* by Laura Lipton and Bruce Wellman (1998) and adapted for the illustrated use in this example.

Bean Activity

Meeting participants are each provided with a plastic bag containing 10–12 beans. Inside the plastic bag is the following set of directions for the activity:

You have been given a bag containing 10–12 beans. Your job is to circulate around the room during the first five minutes of the meeting trying to collect as many beans from other members of our staff as possible. You can only collect beans when you get a fellow staff member to answer a question in a yes/no manner. If you get the member to say "yes" or "no," you can take a bean from his or her bag. If someone gets you to say "yes" or "no," he or she can take a bean from your bag. At the end of our activity time, I will stop the activity and ask you to count the number of beans that you have collected.

As the meeting leader, just hand out the bags, let people know that the directions for the activity are in the bag, and observe people's reactions as they circulate around the room. At the end of five minutes, call "time" and ask people to count the number of beans they collected. The person with the most beans is declared the winner. We normally provide some type of prize for the winner. We have given the winner a large can of pork and beans, which people seem to enjoy. Here are the major steps involved in conducting the bean activity:

- Prepare the bags with the beans and printed instructions in advance; hand them out to team members as they enter the room, and ask them to read the directions and get started with the activity.
- Circulate around the room and observe people in action; call out the time when there is about one minute left in the activity.
- Stop the activity when the time set aside for it has expired.
- Have group members count the number of beans in their bags.
- Ask staff members what they learned about each other as a result of this activity.

There are many variations to the yes/no answers that allow members to take a bean from the bag. Here are some that we have used successfully at school sites:

- Bean Surrender: Have the group members give up a bean if they actually answer the question asked. Tell them to provide an answer to another question, and the originator of the original question must guess the question the new answer fits, or they must give up a bean.
- Questioning Comment: Instead of the yes/no response in the original activity, require activity participants to generate another question when presented with the first question. Participants lose a bean if they don't respond with a question.
- Truth or Lie: After the initial question is posed, the receiver of the question must choose to answer correctly or lie in their response. The originator of the question must decide whether the answer provided by this staff member is true or if it is a lie. If the question originator guesses correctly, this person gets to

take a bean from the question receiver's bag; if he or she guesses incorrectly, a bean is lost.

Group Spelling Bee

This strategy asks people to use both their mental and physical learning capacities as they engage in very energizing activity. The activity works like this:

- The larger group is divided into two teams of equal numbers.
- Each staff member is given a sheet of paper that has a vowel or consonant written on it; each team has the same number and type of sheets.
- The teams line up on opposite sides of the meeting room.
- The leader of the group describes the process of the activity and the rules for participation.
- The leader of the group calls out a word, and the members of the two teams must rearrange themselves to spell out the word; those members holding a letter that is not being used in the current word must stand off to the side.
- The team that correctly spells its word the fastest wins a point.
- At the end of several rounds, the team points are totaled and a winner is declared.

School sites have adapted this activity to meet the needs of their school staff. Some of the variations used to add variety include the following:

- Silent Spelling Bee: This is operated in much the same way as the original activity except that individual team members are asked to spell the words correctly without using verbal communication.
- Math Sentence Building: This variation requires group members to be presented with number cards and mathematical operation cards instead of letter cards. Team members are asked to build a mathematical sentence that yields the number called by the meeting leader. The team that builds the longest number sentence using the most staff members is declared the winner of a round. Multiple rounds may be played.
- Pattern Repeat: Individual staff members are given colored sheets of paper. The meeting leader shows the groups a color pattern on the overhead projector. The teams are asked to copy the pattern using team members. The team with the most correct and fastest solution is declared the winner.

Puzzling Problem

In this activity, staff members are energized by the challenges of doing a movement activity to help them solve a problem. Here is the general outline of how it works:

- The entire staff is divided into smaller teams of three or four members.
- Each team is asked to sit at a table or other flat working surface.
- Each team is provided with a small puzzle that provides some challenge in its completion. Teams have been successful in putting together puzzles of around 100 pieces.
- The teams are asked to put their puzzles together without having any verbal interaction; they must communicate using only signals and gestures.
- The team that completes its puzzle first wins the activity.
- Be sure to ask the team members what they learned as a result of this activity.

There are many different ways that this activity could be used to energize a group. Here are a few ideas:

- Talking Puzzle: This variation is similar to the original activity, but team members are allowed to talk during the puzzle-completion process.
- Mystery Puzzle Solution: Team members are still engaged in solving a puzzle, but in this variation, they are required to put it together face down. This requires that team members focus on the puzzle patterns rather than use the picture on the front as a clue to putting the puzzle together.
- Team Puzzle: At the beginning of the activity, each team is assigned a puzzle, as in the original activity. The members work on the puzzle for a set amount of time, but they are asked to rotate from their original puzzle to a puzzle on their right. They then begin to work on that puzzle until they are asked to rotate to yet another puzzle. The groups continue to rotate until they get to all of the puzzles or until one of the groups completes work on a puzzle during its turn. The group that completes a puzzle is declared the winner.

Let's Make a Deal

This is an icebreaker that can be used to start a faculty meeting. Adults enjoy having door prizes. To add a little life to the meeting, it is fun to play *Let's Make a Deal*. Once a person wins the door prize, you can offer the staff the chance to make a deal. Give the staff member the opportunity to keep the door prize or trade it for an item in a bag, box, or envelope. Once he or she picks the item, say "Let's make a deal!" Have about 20 $1 bills in your hand and offer to buy back the gift. Ask the staff member if he or she is willing to trade the prize for a dollar, then two dollars, three dollars, and so on. You could have some of these items in your bag or box:

Mug

Electric pencil sharpener

Professional book

Stickers

Desk items

Small plant or flower

Game for the classroom

Deck of cards

Markers

Candy

School t-shirt

School hat

Envelope

Lottery ticket

Movie rental coupon

Get-out-of-duty-free pass

$10–$20 gift certificate to buy something for their classroom

Gift certificate to a restaurant or a coffee shop

Your parent organization might be willing to provide you with some door prizes.

Best Poker Hand

In this energizing challenge, team members work together to answer a set of questions on a sheet provided to them. For each correct answer, the team gets to select one card from a standard deck of cards. The team uses the cards to build the best five-card poker hand possible. After all of the teams have finished the challenge, all of the poker hands are evaluated; the team with the best hand is the winner. Here are the steps involved in this activity:

- Each team picks up a question sheet.
- The team has five minutes to write the answers to the questions on this sheet.
- When the teams have finished, they pick up the answer envelope. They correct their answer sheets and count up the number of correct responses.
- Once the teams determine the number of correct responses, they shuffle the standard card deck on their work table.
- The teams select the number of cards corresponding to the number of questions they were able to answer correctly—if they got five answers correct, they could choose five cards.
- Once the cards are chosen, the teams work together to build a winning poker hand. Once their hands are built, they let the meeting leader know the results. The group with the highest poker hand wins the challenge.

Following is a sheet with sample questions you might consider using with this exercise. Feel free to adapt and make changes as necessary.

Summary

In this chapter, we introduced you to a variety of ways to energize your staff at the beginning of meetings. This is just a sample of the many activities that are being used to help team members get energized and connected as they begin the meeting process. These activities are designed to get a good start on the process of energizing. In Chapter 4, "Keeping the Group Engaged," we will examine another whole set of ideas that has been used successfully to keep the energy level high and to keep participants engaged in the meeting. As you complete this chapter, take a few minutes to check your own learning by considering the following:

- Why is it important to begin meetings by shifting your teachers' emotions to the positive?
- What impact can music have in shaping the energy level of a meeting?
- What activities do you see as holding some promise in helping you to energize the start of your staff meetings?
- What did you learn in this chapter that you will implement in your meetings in the future?

Questions for Best Poker Hand

1. List the four U.S. presidents who were assassinated while in office (you must list all four answers to receive credit for a correct answer).

2. List the four railroads on a standard *Monopoly* game board. (You must list all four answers to receive credit for a correct answer.)

3. In music, what does *fortissimo* mean?

4. On the periodic table of the elements, what is the atomic symbol for gold?

5. In mathematics, how many sides does a hexagon have?

6. In speech, what term is given to words that join words, phrases, or clauses?

7. Which impressionist painted *Starry Night*?

8. The Olympic biathlon event combines which two sports?

9. What is the capital city of Canada?

10. Which weighs more: a ton of bricks or a ton of feathers?

4

Keeping the
Group Engaged

I think that education is power. I think that being able to communicate with people is power. One of my main goals on this planet is to encourage people to empower themselves.

—Oprah Winfrey

Now that you have gained the group's attention, what do you do next? This question has caused many meeting leaders sleepless nights as they plan to conduct a meeting. An energized staff meeting has a great start, but it also keeps people's minds engaged as it progresses. This crucial part of the meeting is often overlooked, but it can make all the difference in the world in the total success of the group's experience together.

As you read this chapter, look for the following ideas to guide you as you work to keep your group members engaged and productive through that difficult middle stage of a staff meeting:

- Why it is important to maximize the engagement of a group of people during a meeting
- The power of personal and professional stories to keep a group engaged

- Specific participation strategies that work to engage the minds of those attending your meeting
- Ways to build your staff's capacity to take responsibility for staying engaged in meeting content
- Simple but powerful techniques to assess the engagement of a group during a meeting and intervention strategies to get them back on track when their minds wander

Using Personal and Professional Stories

Stories can magically provide your meetings with warmth and energy, or they can set a negative and low tone that is very difficult to overcome. What makes the difference? Let's examine some of the ways that leaders who are able to energize their meetings use stories to set and maintain a great tone throughout the meeting.

The Story Context

Good energizing stories "fit into" a group. The members of a staff can relate to these kinds of stories; they tend to motivate us and entertain us as well. Good energizing stories relate to things that teachers are interested in at their school. These stories resonate with the staff. Read the following story that we heard a leader share at a recent meeting and think about how it related to the teachers at the meeting:

In getting ready to start our meeting today, I would like to share something that I heard at our parent–teacher conferences the other day. Mrs. (name omitted) stopped me in the hall and shared with me that she had recently finished her conferences about her three children. She talked about how all of the teachers at this school really knew her children and worked hard to help make them successful. She commented that over the years, her children had been taught by just about every teacher at this school, but her experience was always the same; everyone did what was best for her children. She said that she just stopped to thank me and asked that I pass the thanks on to you, the teachers.

This kind of story can be very motivating to the teachers because it appeals to their sense of purpose: making a difference in the lives of children.

Other stories provide context in different ways. See how the following story with a different twist added energy to a meeting:

Before we start today, I'd like to share a story with you. I was in a classroom the other day when a student raised his hand to answer and got a little carried away. He struggled so hard to raise his hand that all of the buttons on his shirt popped off and his shirt opened up, exposing his t-shirt. He looked at the teacher, who was thinking that he might be embarrassed, and said "Hey, I'm Superman." The whole class and the teacher burst out laughing. So much for feeling embarrassed!

The teachers started to laugh when the punch line of this story was told. They all could relate to the student and the teacher. The rest of the meeting was productive and energizing.

The Story Content

The content of the story should be short and to the point. Stories that go on forever tend to zap the energy out of a group of teachers. Keep the content focused and on track. Include as many details as necessary to help people get the meaning of the story, but don't dwell on insignificant parts of the story that tend to bore people. The content should be interesting and pertinent to the teachers' lives. Stories about school happenings, locally based content, or content that is personally related to the teachers can be very motivating and engaging.

As you read the following story that was recently shared at a staff meeting, think about how the content of the story worked to "hook" the staff members emotionally into the meeting.

In starting our meeting today, I would like to share a story that I recently read about a group of teachers who faced challenges similar to those that we are facing this year. Think about how we might use their experiences as we begin to tackle the issues that we face.

In this particular high school, the students were having lots of trouble reading their textbooks. The teachers met and talked about the possible reasons for this problem. A segment of the staff said that they thought the real reason the students were having trouble in school was that many of them were too lazy to read their books. The staff was ready to end the conversation there when several of the teachers brought up the fact that according to the results of recent testing, a large percentage of the students had reading levels lower than what was required to be successful with the textbooks. Having this information helped the teachers to begin to generate specific interventions, such as providing audiotapes for the students to check out, a parent tutoring program to help explain the reading material, and a reading café where students could go for help with reading in their content areas. As these ideas began to get attention, several of the teachers began to look at the problem differently; they started to see that, at least in some cases, the students had little control over their success in reading within their subject-area texts. Several of the teachers started to see that they needed to make modifications for the students rather than just expect to have the students come up to their level of instruction; they began to see things from the students' perspective rather than just asking the students to see things from the teacher's perspective.

Take a minute and talk in small groups about what you heard in the story that might help us as we begin to tackle the attendance problem that we are having at our school.

This story may sound very simple, but it asked the teachers to look outside their world and to examine a problem from another perspective. Many times, our teachers get stuck and only look at the problem facing them. It can be energizing for them to use their problem-solving skills to examine how others have solved similar problems or even to generate a solution to a case study that is outside their normal situation. It is easier for teachers to develop their problem-solving skills by looking at other situations because they have no emotional investment in the solution. We have used this technique effectively to help our teachers build their problem-solving skills and to energize our staff meetings. In the end, you will need to help your teachers transfer what they learned from your story to their own situation.

Points to Keep in Mind When Using Stories to Help Staff Members Connect

When using stories to energize and build your teachers' skills in problem solving, keep the following points in mind:

- Keep the story brief and to the point.
- Let teachers know up front why you are telling the story and what you hope they will learn from it.
- Make sure that the context of the story is related to the work your teachers do or connects to their experiences.
- Keep in mind what may motivate your staff—share positives that you see in the building or hear as you talk with parents and teachers about the school.

- Keep a notebook or journal handy as you walk around the school so that as you hear motivating and energizing stories, you can write them down to share when appropriate.
- Vary your use of this energizer so that it does not become monotonous.

Specific Strategies and Techniques to Keep People's Minds Engaged During the Entire Meeting

Carouseling

A highly effective and energizing activity involves carouseling to generate information. In carouseling, the leader gets maximum participation from the people at the meeting. Here is how the basic concept of carouseling works:

- The large group is divided into smaller teams of four to six people.
- The team is assigned a task that must be completed within 8–10 minutes; the results of their work should be written on chart paper that is stationed at locations throughout the room.
- At the end of the work time, the group leader directs the members to designate about half of the team as "travelers" and the other half as "stayers."
- The group leader tells the participants that the team members designated as travelers will move to other teams during the activity; those designated as stayers will stay at their charts.
- The group leader tells the participants that the stayers will stay at their charts and explain the work that their team did during the work time; the travelers will move on to another group, listen to the stayer's explanation, and then add the information to their chart.
- Normally, the travelers move one chart clockwise and remain there until a signal is given by the group leader. A signal is normally given after two to three minutes of work time between the travelers and the stayers.
- The group leader has the travelers rotate three or four times to new groups and then asks them to return to their original or "home" group. At this point, those who traveled and those who stayed talk about what they learned during this process.

After reading these directions, you still may be a little confused about how to implement this activity. Here is an example in which John used carouseling as a way to help a group brainstorm ideas. The example is written using John's own language:

Today, we'll use an activity called *carouseling* to generate examples for the standards by which we will be developing portfolios. Divide yourselves into groups of six. [Participants did.]

Designate one of your members to come up and pick up a piece of chart paper and some markers. [Participants did.]

Each of your charts contains the title of one of the standards we will use in developing our portfolios. Your job as a group is to write one simple, straightforward statement that clarifies the meaning of your standard. Once this is in place, your group needs to work together to generate at least four examples of artifacts that could be used to illustrate the standards you have been given. Your group has 10 minutes to do both of these tasks. What questions do you have about the process? Go. [The small groups worked on the task for 10 minutes.]

Stop what you are working on. In your teams of six, designate half of your group as "travelers" and the other half as "stayers." The stayers will stay at the chart and explain the work of the group on the standards; the travelers will move to other groups on my signal and listen to the explanation that is provided by the stayers. Once their explanation is over, you need to provide any clarification that is needed for their statement related to the standard plus add two new examples to their list of examples of artifacts. The travelers need to actually write these items on the charts they are visiting with their own marker. Go ahead and divide yourselves in to stayer and traveler groups." [Group members do.]

Let's see the hands of the stayers. [Individuals raise hands.] Let's see the hands of the travelers. [Individuals raise hands.] Travelers will move one group clockwise at the signal of go. You will work there for two to three minutes. When you hear music playing, it is time to move one more group clockwise. As soon as the music stops, start to work with the new group you have just joined in the same manner as the last group that you just left; you will have two to three minutes to work in this group. When you hear music playing, stop your activity and move one more group clockwise. Repeat this pattern until I give you further directions. [John starts the groups with a "go" signal; after two to three minutes, he plays a song, and the travelers move one group clockwise and continue the process. After three rotations, John stops the process and has the travelers go back to their home groups and gives the following direction.]

Return to your home group and talk about what you have learned in the process; travelers, share what you saw on the other charts as you traveled around; stayers, share what you learned from those who visited your chart. Be ready to share your learning with the entire group in three to five minutes.

Carouseling can be used for a variety of purposes. Here are some examples:

- Brainstorming ideas from common topic areas
- Brainstorming ideas from a variety of topic areas
- Generating a pro–con list
- Clarifying topics
- Generating questions
- Generating answers to questions
- Helping a group to simplify a complex topical area

Energizing Strategies for Setting Priorities

An important task of any group or team is to set priorities for the ideas to be discussed or the work that needs to be completed. Here are some ideas that we have used in our work with groups of staff members over the years.

Buy What Is Most Important

This strategy, although simple in nature, provides an energizing way to help staff member groups to set priorities for tasks and ideas. It works like this:

- At the beginning of the meeting, provide each staff member with a set amount of play money. Think about what you want them to prioritize, then issue the combination of play money that will help them narrow their choices.
- Let the staff members know that after a discussion of all possible ideas or strategies to be explored at the meeting, they will have a chance to bid on their top two choices from the list generated through the discussion.
- Put all of the possible solutions on a chart tablet and ask staff members to think about their top choices for implementation from the list.
- Ask staff members to place their money in envelopes that have been attached to the chart near the choices.
- At the end of the "buying period," count the amount of money in each envelope. The top "money getters" are the prioritized choices; those with the lowest amounts of money are eliminated from the list.

There are many ways to vary this activity. You are limited only by your creativity and your ability to try new things with your staff members to keep this activity energizing and fun. Here are some of the most common variations of this idea that we have seen or implemented:

- Auction: Hold an auction to determine the most important tasks. The leader of the meeting acts as the auctioneer and conducts an open auction to see which ideas get the most money or interest.
- Credit Card Bidding: Instead of issuing money to teachers, provide each staff member with an amount of credit to be used in the bidding process. Allow staff members to trade and exchange their credits to prioritize the tasks.
- Hidden Costs: Place the choices to be prioritized on tables or on charts around the room. Have staff members talk about the hidden costs of the different tasks listed; some of the choices may require more capital to implement. When staff members are asked to place bids on the items, they must take into account the hidden costs of the tasks. Those items with more hidden costs will need a larger bid to be selected. For example, a choice with more hidden costs may take a minimum bid of $5 from each interested party, whereas an idea with minimal hidden costs may take a minimum of bid of only $1 from each interested party.
- Group Bidding: After all of the ideas have been presented and posted, allow staff members a chance to get together in teams and combine their money as a group to "purchase" their top choices. It is important to be careful with this strategy to avoid allowing groups to bid against each other and causing hard feelings.

It's a Star

When any group of staff members is asked to generate a list of possible solutions to a problem or to develop the next steps in a planning process, some of the ideas carry more importance than others. This energizer allows teachers to see that certain items need to have a higher level of consideration than others. Here is how it works:

- The team members generate a list of possible ideas or solutions to a problem.
- Once all of the possible ideas are listed, team members are asked to clarify any ideas or items on the list that the group does not understand.

- Once everyone understands all of the ideas, the group members are given large gold stars; one star has a "5" written on it, another has a "4" written on it, and a third has a "3" written on it. In addition to these three stars, each team member is also given three stars that have no numbers.
- The leader of the group asks all of the team members to stand up and put the 5 star on the idea that is their top choice, the 4 star by their second choice, and the 3 star by their third choice. They can place their unnumbered stars by any of the possible choices.
- Once everyone has had a chance to place their stars, the leader reports the results; the group members now hold a discussion about their thoughts in relation to the activity.
- Once the discussion is finished, the group leader asks team members if any of them would like to move their stars. Any who are interested in moving their stars are given the opportunity to do so.
- The group engages in another discussion about the process and the results of their star placement; the group makes a decision about the prioritization of the items on their list.

Criteria Rating

In this variation of It's a Star, team members are asked to rate the ideas generated during a group process, but they are required to use agreed-upon criteria to use in their ratings. By developing a clear and objective rating system, team members think about the needs of the problem when looking at possible solutions. In our work with groups over the years, we have found that teachers can benefit from evaluating possible choices against clear criteria. Once you help them to develop this kind of thinking, you will find that their solutions become well thought out and focused. The activity works like this:

- Have your team members develop a list of possible ideas or solutions by brainstorming.
- Allow them time to ask for clarification of any items from the list that are unclear.
- Tell the teachers they will have a chance to prioritize their ideas, but first, you want them to develop the criteria they will use in this prioritization process.
- Ask teachers to work in small groups to generate a list of criteria they will use to prioritize their choices. Provide them with some starter ideas, such as the impact on the school's mission, the cost of implementation, short-term versus long-term ideas, easy to implement versus hard to implement, etc.

- Have each small group write its prioritization criteria on another chart tablet or whiteboard; once all of the groups have written their ideas down, hold a discussion about which criteria the group thinks will best help them to prioritize their list.
- Ask the team members to use the stars they have been given to rate the possible ideas or solutions using the same process as described in the It's a Star activity.
- Once all of the ideas have been rated, engage the teachers in a discussion about the process and the results. Be sure they use the criteria they developed to rate the choices in their discussions.
- Develop a plan to move forward on the top choices of the group members.

Pair Basketball

At times, teacher teams may have difficulty talking and listening to each other. This energizer is designed to help people do both in a fun way. It only takes a minute to set up and implement, but it provides fun and energy and helps teachers to develop important communication skills. Here is how it works:

- Divide your teachers into pair groups using a random strategy.
- Have the pairs stand facing each other in a circle (see Figure 4.1).
- Ask team members to designate a Person A and a Person B in each pair.
- Place paper grocery sacks about three feet behind each of the team members on the outside of the circle.
- Provide each team member with four balls (these could be tennis balls, ping-pong balls, or even paper wads).
- The person who is facing the sack (Person A) gives the person who has his or her back to the sack (Person B) specific directions about how to throw the ball over his or her head to make it into the sack. Person B needs to shoot the ball over his or her back without looking at the sack.
- Person A watches the first shot and then gives Person B specific directions about how to improve the accuracy of the next shot. Person B attempts the second shot; the process continues until all four shots have been taken.
- The team members reverse roles: Person A becomes the shooter and Person B gives directions.
- The team with the most shots in the sack after two rounds is declared the winner.

Figure 4.1   Pair Basketball

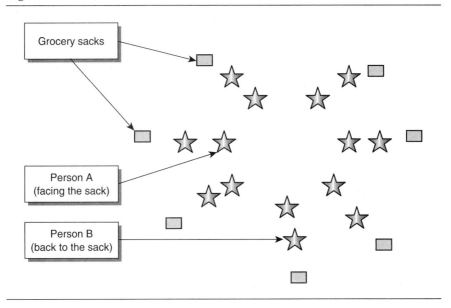

There are many ways that you can offer teachers variations of the listening and communicating skills that this activity provides. Here are several that you may consider using in working with your team members.

- Blindfolded Pair Basketball: In this variation, Person B wears a blindfold and faces the sack. In our work with teacher teams, we have found that people can be uncomfortable wearing blindfolds, but allowing them to shoot forward can make the activity easier to do. You will need to assess your teachers' comfort level in deciding exactly how to complete this activity.
- General to Specific: A fun variation of the pair basketball activity is to have the assistance given to the shooter start off as general and become more specific. You can either use the backward-facing or the blindfolded method to ensure that the shooter does not see the sack or target. Here is how this one works:

    In the first round, Person A can give Person B only general feedback about his or her efforts. The feedback can only be "yes" (you made it) or "no" (you didn't make it).

    During the second round, Person A can give Person B more specific directions. This information might consist of giving the person feedback about his or her effort and one statement of advice for the next shot. The information may sound like this: "You missed to the left by about 10 inches; for the next shot, move your hand a little to the left to make it in the basket."

In the third round of the game, Person A can hold a short conference about the shot to give specific improvement information to Person B. A conference may sound like this: "On your last shot, you were almost there, but you missed the basket by about 10 inches to the left. For this shot, move your hand a little to the left. Take a minute and, without the ball, practice your release, and I'll watch you as you do to see if you are on target."

After the pairs go through all three rounds, ask them to talk about the difference in their communication and results in the three rounds.

Progressive Problem Solving

This activity is unique because team members build on each other's ideas and solutions. The activity works like this:

- Divide the large group into smaller teams of three to four people.
- Designate a Team 1, Team 2, etc., until all the teams have a number.
- Share the problem in a written form with Team 1. This team has two minutes to read the problem and generate a possible solution.
- Once the two minutes have elapsed, Team 1 needs to pass its problem and solution to Team 2; this team has three minutes to read and understand the problem and the solution generated by Team 1. It must add two possible solutions to the list of ideas.
- Once the three minutes have elapsed, Team 2 must pass the sheet to Team 3; this group must read and understand the problem and the solutions generated by the other teams. Team 3 has four minutes to add three possible solutions to the list of ideas generated by the other teams.
- The process is repeated until all of the teams have had a chance to add ideas to the original list.
- The original list is given back to Team 1, all of the ideas on the list are discussed as a large group, and the most desirable solutions are selected by the large group.

The basic idea of progressive problem solving can be built on in a variety of ways. A few are listed here:

- Multiple Progressive Problem Solving: This variation is similar to the original idea, but all of the groups are given a problem to start the process. As the papers are passed on in a circular manner, all of the groups do Step 2, Step 3, and so on, until all of the papers have circulated to all of the groups. You will generate solutions for a number of problems simultaneously.
- Multiple-Perspectives Problem Solving: In this activity, each of the groups is given a role it must assume in generating their ideas. For example, Group 1 may be assigned to examine the problem from the school faculty perspective, Group 2 may be assigned to examine the problem only from the community's perspective, and the remaining groups may be assigned other important perspectives that need to be considered in making the final decision. You, as the leader, or the staff members can decide which perspectives need to be considered by the teams.
- Questions Problem Solving: In this variation, the initial group generates solutions to the problem and passes its paper to the next group. The next group examines the problem and the ideas the first team generated, but this group can only ask questions about the ideas generated by the first team. The second team has two minutes to complete this process and then passes the paper back to the group that generated the original solutions and ideas. Then the first group must address the questions generated by the second team and refine their original ideas. This team is given five minutes to complete this process, and then it must pass its refinements back to the second team, which examines their ideas. If the second team still has questions, it writes them down and passes their questions back to the original group. This process helps groups to refine their suggestions early in the problem-solving process.

From My Perspective

An important aspect of problem solving is looking at a problem from multiple perspectives. When teams can do this, they are able to anticipate some of the situations that normally cause problems during the initial stages of implementation. This activity uses a graphic that helps team members examine the problem and its solutions from a variety of perspectives. In implementing this activity, use a chart similar to the one illustrated in Figure 4.2.

- Post a clear description of the problem faced by the group or the organization in the center of the chart.
- Around the outside of the chart, list the different perspectives that need to be considered in generating solutions and ideas.
- One at a time, list the unique needs of each perspective and then list the possible solutions that might be generated by a group with this perspective.
- After all of the perspectives have been addressed, talk about the possible solutions that the staff members need to adopt to address the concern or problem.

Go to the Four Corners

During meetings, at times a whole-group discussion can become stale and dry. Group members may benefit from a chance to meet in small groups to talk more in depth about specific parts of an issue. In this activity, you, as the leader, can send your team members to corners to energize the group and to allow in-depth discussions. Here is an example of how a leader recently used this strategy to energize her group:

Norma, a principal, asked her teachers to talk in a large group about plans for an open house that was scheduled for a month from the meeting date. After about five minutes of discussion, the teachers ran out of ideas for the open house. Norma divided the staff into four small groups and asked them to go to the four corners of the room and talk about the open house for five minutes. As the small groups moved to the corners, Norma started to notice that the level of conversation rose and the room was filled with planning noise. After the five minutes were up, she asked each of the teams to return to the large group and share the ideas they generated. To Norma's delight, 10 new ideas were generated as a result of this energizing activity.

This energizer can be implemented simply and quickly. It is also easy to vary its design. Here are a few ideas to get you started in adapting it to fit your group's needs:

Figure 4.2 From My Perspective

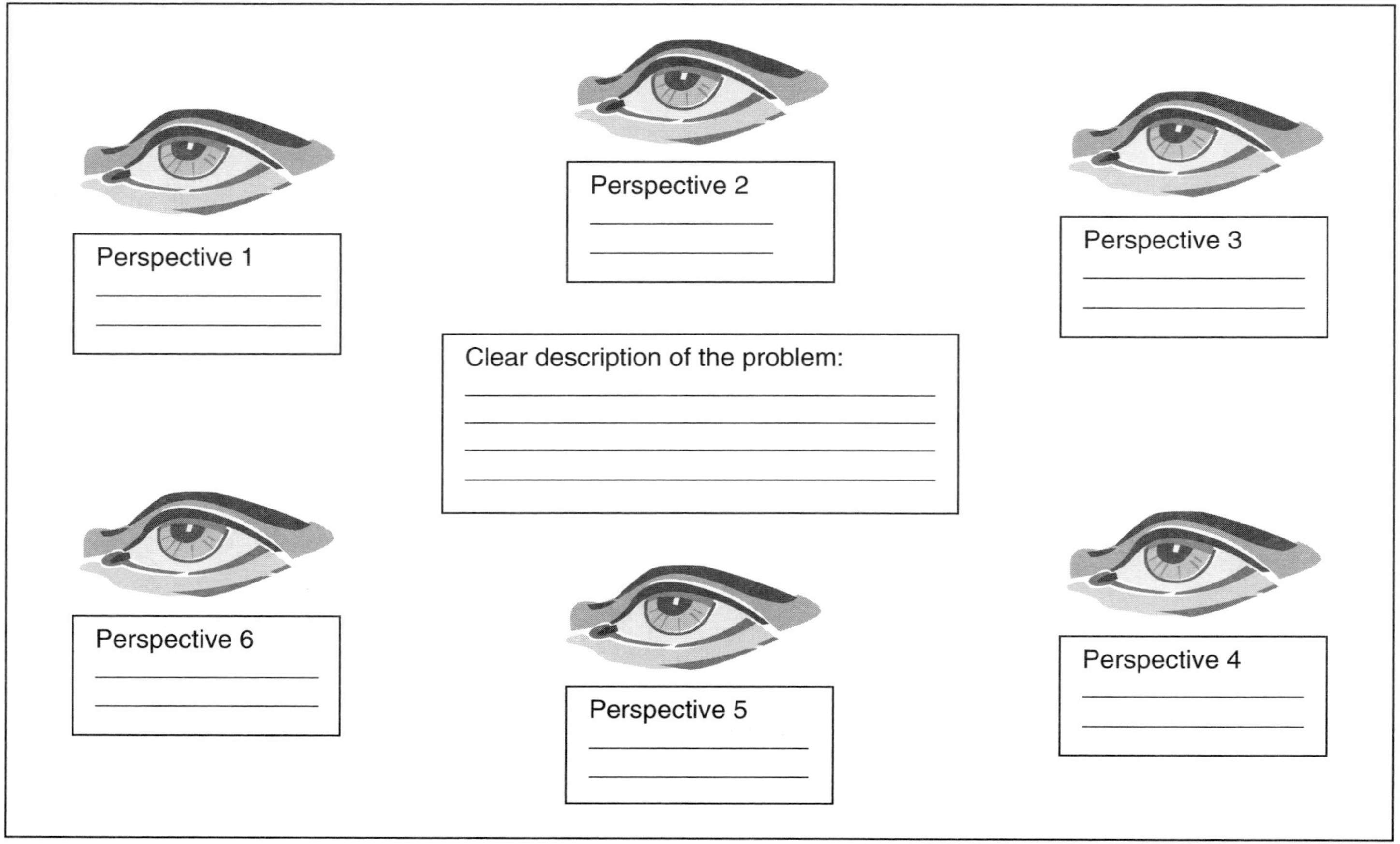

Perspective 3

Perspective 4

Perspective 2

Clear description of the problem:

Perspective 5

Perspective 1

Perspective 6

- Corner Perspectives: As you send each group to a corner of the room, assign them a unique perspective that they need to consider as they hold their discussion. Here are some of the perspectives that you can ask the small groups to consider:

     School district's perspective

     Parents' perspective

     Students' perspective

     Teachers' perspective

     Impact on the community

     Impact on local businesses

     Positive aspects of the problem

     Negative aspects of the problem

     Economic cost of the solutions

     Time costs of the solutions

     Worst-case scenarios

     Best-case scenarios

     If we do nothing

     Holes in the solutions

     Whole problem

     Details of the problem

     Causes of the problem

     Ripple effects of the possible solutions

     Others, as appropriate

- Corner Volunteers: Instead of asking everyone to go to the corners, in this variation, you can send a small group of volunteers to work on a problem resolution. As this small group of volunteers works on the solution, the rest of the group continues with the regular meeting. Once the volunteer group finishes its task, it stops the large-group meeting and reports its progress and ideas. The large group then acts on its recommendations.
- Get Out of the Corner: In this variation, each group is assigned to work in a corner on a specific part of a larger task. A goal is set for all of the groups, and each is given a chart tablet to write

down their ideas and solutions. When a group reaches its goal, the members shout "We are out!" and run to the center of the meeting room. Prizes are awarded to the groups that get out of the corner first, second, etc. All of the groups talk about what they learned as a result of this process and how the energizing activity helped to increase their ideas and solutions.

Part-Full or Part-Empty

Many times, educators look at and focus on the negative aspects of a problem. This negative view can limit their ability to generate creative solutions to the problems they face as a staff. This energizer is designed to help teacher teams to balance the positives and negatives of the problem or challenge they are facing. It works like this:

- At the beginning of the problem-resolution process, the leader puts up a chart that shows a drawing of a glass (see Figure 4.3).
- The group is asked to use sticky notepads to write down the positive and negative aspects of the problem facing them or the school. Only one idea can be written on each notepad.
- Teachers are randomly asked to come up to the chart and place one sticky note on either the positive or negative part of the large glass.
- The positive aspects or conditions of the problem are placed on the top part of the glass; the negative aspects or conditions of the problem are placed at the bottom of the glass.
- Once all of the sticky notes have been placed on the large glass, the leader reviews the notes and asks the teachers to discuss what they learned about the problem and what they want to do as a result of the activity.

The following activities are variations of the Part-Full or Part-Empty activity:

- Ask teachers to place sticky notes with one positive and one negative aspect of the issue or problem on the chart. They should place these sticky notes on the chart in an alternating fashion (first a positive note, then a negative note, alternating positive and negative with every other note). This process continues until no more attributes from either the positive or negative side of the issue can be posted; at this point, all posting must stop. This variation requires teams to look at both the positive and negative sides of an issue. In our experience,

Figure 4.3   Part-Full or Part-Empty

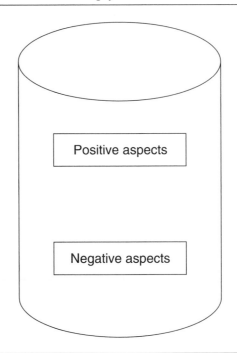

people find it easier to generate the negative aspects of a topic or idea. By requiring them to balance the positive and negative, they are forced to generate positive attributes. This not only keeps the issue balanced but also helps the team develop the habit of looking at both sides of an issue. It pays dividends in the long term for teams.

- Have the team members generate sticky notes for the positive and negative aspects of the problem. Ask team members to place all of the negative aspects on the chart. Next, move to the positive aspects. For every positive aspect or idea placed on the chart, a negative can be removed. The activity is completed when all of the positive aspects have replaced the negative aspects. This variation forces people to move beyond the negative aspects of a situation and begin to look at both the positives and negatives of an issue or idea.

- Duplicate small versions of the large glass chart. Ask individuals or small groups to complete these smaller versions and then have the small groups combine into larger teams to talk about their products. Place the results of their discussions on the larger glass chart. Hold a large-group discussion about the process and the results of working through the exercise. This variation can be helpful because it can defuse the negative emotions that can build up in a large group. Because small teams complete the activity first and then work in larger teams to combine and clarify their thoughts, many of the issues can be dealt with before they get to the large group. This activity also allows more interaction and participation by all team members. Many times, we have found that when a negative idea comes up at the small-group level, a team member tends to present the positive side of the issue. This can be much more effective than letting negative ideas come up in a large-group meeting and asking the leader to help the group see the positive aspects of the situation.

- Have team members generate sticky notes for the positive and negative aspects of the problem or situation facing them. Once all of the ideas have been posted, ask the group to divide itself into small teams to generate ideas to remove the negative aspects from the chart. For an idea to be removed from the chart, the small group must write a specific plan or strategy for its removal. Assign point values to the negative aspects and award teams points for the aspects they are able to remove from the chart. The team with the most points is declared the winner. This variation puts the responsibility for generating solutions on the group and gives members good practice in developing ideas for problem resolution. This practice can pay off down the road as group members tackle more difficult situations.

Compare the Possibilities

Some staff members may benefit from actually seeing ideas written on a board or a chart tablet. In this activity, the meeting leader constructs a table that is used to compare the possible solutions to a problem or the ideas generated by the group. In the table, the general characteristics that will be used to compare the ideas are written and the group's task is to complete the table. Here are the specifics of the activity:

- The leader engages the group members in brainstorming possible solutions to problems or ideas related to the task that the group has been assigned.
- Once the list has been clarified and everyone understands the ideas, the group is asked to list a set of criteria they will use to compare these ideas.
- A table or matrix is written on chart paper on a writing board.
- The leader lists the ideas in the first vertical column of the chart and the brainstormed comparison criteria in the top horizontal row on the chart (see Figure 4.4).

- The team members are asked to talk and compare the ideas using the criteria listed in the top row of the table.
- Once all of the ideas have been compared, the group members are asked to select their top choices.

Parking Lot

Sometimes people will share an idea or concern during a meeting that is not directly connected to the topic currently being discussed. In these situations, the leader normally has to let the person sharing the off-task idea know that his or her suggestion does not match the current discussion. This can lower the energy level of the group. To keep the group energized, it is important to provide group members a place to put their off-topic questions or suggestions. The "parking lot" can be a great instrument to make this happen.

Most leaders designate the parking lot as an area on chart paper or on a side board where people can place their ideas, questions, or concerns about issues so that they do not get in the way of the group's processing of solutions or ideas. See how Jonathan uses this concept in the following example:

Figure 4.4   Generic Comparison Chart

Ideas for consideration ↓	Comparison criterion 1	Comparison criterion 2	Comparison criterion 3	Comparison criterion 4
Idea 1				
Idea 2				
Idea 3				
Idea 4				
Idea 5				

Figure 4.5   Example of a Completed Comparison Table

Ideas for consideration	Cost to budget	Time required to implement	Impact on the students	Perception of the community
Hold school four days per week	Savings of $25,000	Can implement by fall	Learning will be compressed; some students will get tired. Classes will be more intense. Some will be unsupervised on fifth day each week.	Parents will need to make day care arrangements; community may think time is not well spent on day off. Local businesses may not like students free on fifth day.
Use community volunteers	Training $2,000	Three months, including recruitment and training	More adults in the classroom; students can get more help	People will see the challenges the school faces; sense of involvement by the community
Raise user fees	Will raise approximately $25,000	Next school year because of notification	Some may not be able to participate in activities	School activities should be free; raising fees will upset parents
Raise class sizes	$65,000 savings	Fall	Students will get less attention; achievement may fall, classroom-management concerns could rise.	Community may not like larger class sizes
Team teaching	$65,000	Fall	Students would get two teachers in the room working with them; fewer students would slip through the cracks	Community may see this as an advantage to have two teachers working together; parents may not like larger class size or having to connect with two different teachers

In our meeting today, we need to generate a list of ideas for improving our students' math achievement. When we have had this discussion in the past, our group has been taken off task by some issues that people have presented that do not match the content of student achievement in math. Many of the issues people have brought up are extremely valuable, and we want to make sure that they get resolved at some point. Today, rather than talk about them in our math meeting, we will place all off-task responses or questions on the side chart here. The side chart will be called a "parking lot," and it is a place where presently unused vehicles are stored for later use. When the time is appropriate, these vehicles will be brought back into use.

Our parking lot is the same as a vehicle parking lot. Any ideas or comments that come out in the discussion that don't match the current topic will be placed in the parking lot. Once we complete our main topic, we will come back and deal with these statements. It is important to remember that even though they are placed in the parking lot, they are important and will be addressed at a later time.

In this example, Jonathan had thought through how he was planning to introduce the concept of the parking lot. He followed these guidelines:

- Introduce the idea before you experience a lot of off-track behavior; this helps you set the tone that it is important to stay on track. This strategy allows you to take a proactive stance and lets teachers know that you are really interested in their ideas and concerns.
- Remind the group members that just because their ideas are placed in a parking lot, the importance of their thoughts has not been diminished.
- Place the parking lot off to one side of the main board or presentation area. Some leaders even place their parking lot chart in the back of the room. By keeping the parking lot out of the front of the room, you don't allow it to become the focal point of the meeting.
- Some principals will write the ideas that come up during the meeting in the parking lot; others place a marker in the general vicinity and ask teachers to write in their own parking lot statements on the chart paper. Do what works best for you.
- When statements are placed in the parking lot, the leader should let the teachers know when they will be addressed. Good times to address parking lot issues are before breaks, before lunch, and

the end of the day. We have found that addressing these issues when time is constrained keeps people moving forward more quickly than if you select a part of the day when there is unlimited time or take time away from more valuable topics. We sometimes use all three time periods and address a few items on the list during each period. This helps to address the items but doesn't bog down the group in looking at many issues at once.

Clarification Only

When new ideas are suggested, teachers can sometimes throw a monkey wrench into the works when they are too quick to negate an idea or agree with it before hearing other suggestions. Monkey wrenches can cause the group to quickly lose energy. The strategy of "clarification only" can help to energize a group by making sure that the group only clarifies an issue or idea before the members make up their minds. It works like this:

- The group members first engage in a session in which they brainstorm a lot of ideas to help solve the problem facing the group. No comments, positive or negative, are allowed during this phase of the process.
- Once all of the possible ideas are listed, the leader tells group members that they can only ask clarifying questions about the suggestions listed on the chart.
- In some situations, the leader may need to model some clarifying questions rather than allow the group to decide. You may consider the following guidelines to help the group understand the critical attributes of true clarifying questions:

  Clarifying questions allow the group to go deeper in their understanding of the idea or suggestion.

  Clarifying questions avoid placing value on an idea or suggestion.

  The person generating the clarifying question needs to be sincere in his or her desire to learn more about the idea or suggestion.

  The question needs to be worded in a positive manner.

Here are some sample clarifying questions a group may consider:

  Tell me more about the idea of . . .

  Please give me more details about . . .

What are the specifics of . . .

How do you see this being implemented in . . .

What would be the substeps of . . .

What specific details about _____ can you provide?

I don't understand_____. Please provide clarification on . . .

- One person at a time is allowed to ask a clarifying question; the person who gave the initial idea is given a chance to provide the clarification.
- The process continues until all of the clarifying questions about an idea or suggestion have been addressed.
- Once all of the original ideas have been explored and clarified, the group can begin the process of prioritizing the suggested ideas or solutions for final implementation.

See the Ripple Effects

Normally, school-based teams don't always consider the external impact of their decisions. This activity can energize the group and allows members a chance to consider all of the "ripple effects" of their decisions. The use of a visual tool also helps to energize a group of people and allow them to see the impact of their possible decisions. A sample of a chart that we have used with groups is depicted in Figure 4.6.

We find that the visual representation of the potential effects of the group's decisions or actions allows teachers to really see the results of their decisions. You don't have to be a great artist to draw a chart such as this. We usually draw our charts so that the ripples are not evenly spaced from the center or cause. This is purposeful because we want the team members to know that the ripple effects for certain groups or individuals may come at different times or distances from the event or action. Here is a brief summary of how the process of understanding ripple effects normally works:

- Have the group members generate a list of possible ideas or problem solutions.
- Work with the group to narrow the list down to two or three ideas that may have some merit in solving the problem.
- Using one chart for each suggestion or idea, write the idea or suggestion in the center space.

Figure 4.6 See the Ripple Effects

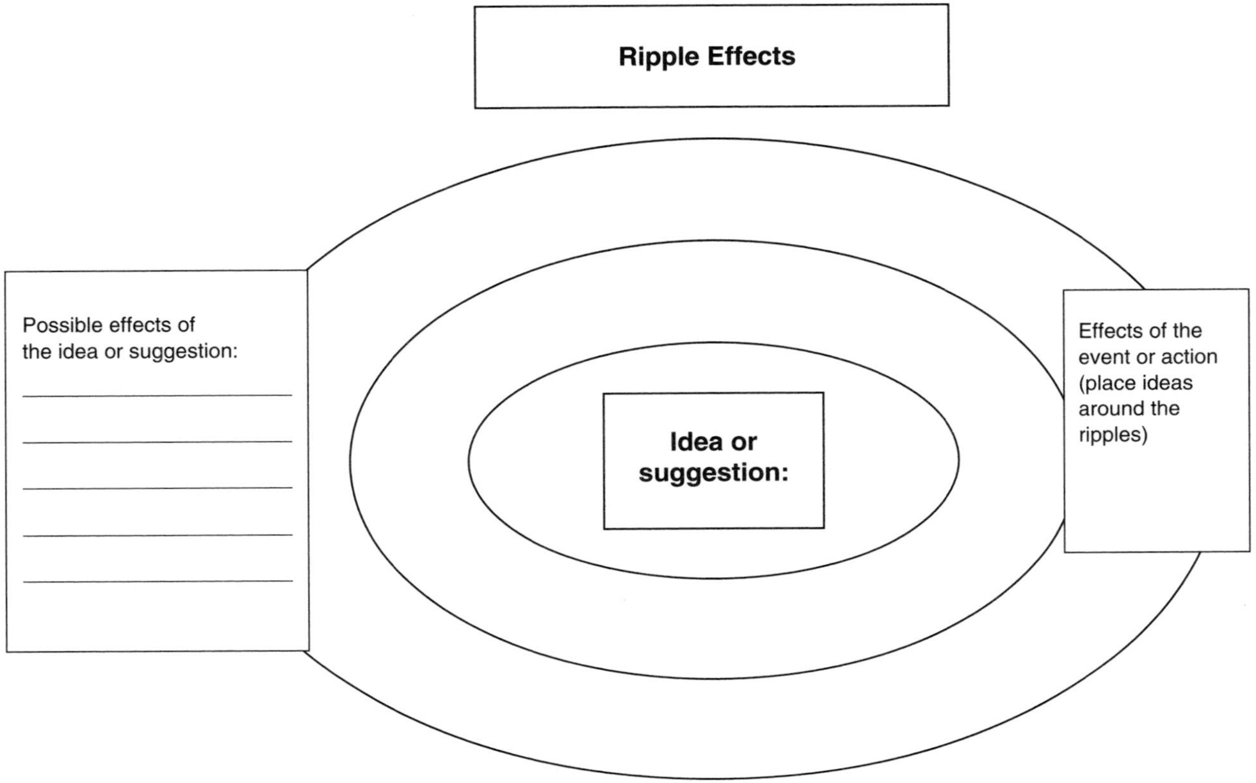

Ripple Effects

Effects of the event or action (place ideas around the ripples)

Idea or suggestion:

Possible effects of the idea or suggestion:

- Engage the group members in brainstorming all of the possible effects of the suggestion or idea. The group leader should write these effects in the box in the lower-left corner of the chart.
- Once all of the potential effects have been listed, have the group members discuss where they should be placed on the main chart; the distance from the center represents how quickly the ripple effect would be felt or the relative strength of the idea or suggestion on the affected party.
- After the whole group has had a chance to analyze the ripple effects, hold a dialogue about what the group learned in the process and what they want to do. This is a process that can be guided by the leader of the group.

A group of teachers whom Sheila recently led through this process developed the ripple effects depicted in Figure 4.7. Only a sample of the ripple effects identified are included in the example.

This general idea can be adapted to fit a variety of needs and situations. Here are some of the ideas that others have used in the past to make this strategy fit the needs of their staff members.

- Small-Group Ripple Effects: A simple variation of the large-group identification involves breaking the large group into smaller teams to talk about the relative impact of the ideas or suggestions. Here are the details:

  The larger group is divided into smaller teams consisting of two or three people each.

  Each of these smaller teams is given a copy of the ripple effects chart and asked to generate a set of effects and to place them on the "ripples" in relation to their impact. All of the small teams work from the same idea or suggestion.

  Each small team completes a chart; once all of the groups have finished, the small teams combine into larger groups to have a dialogue about their ideas and placements.

  The entire group comes back together in a large group to talk about the ideas generated and the processing that occurred in the smaller groups.

  The large group uses the information that was generated during the activity to make decisions regarding the implementation of the ideas or suggestions generated.

Figure 4.7   Example of a Completed Ripple Effects Chart

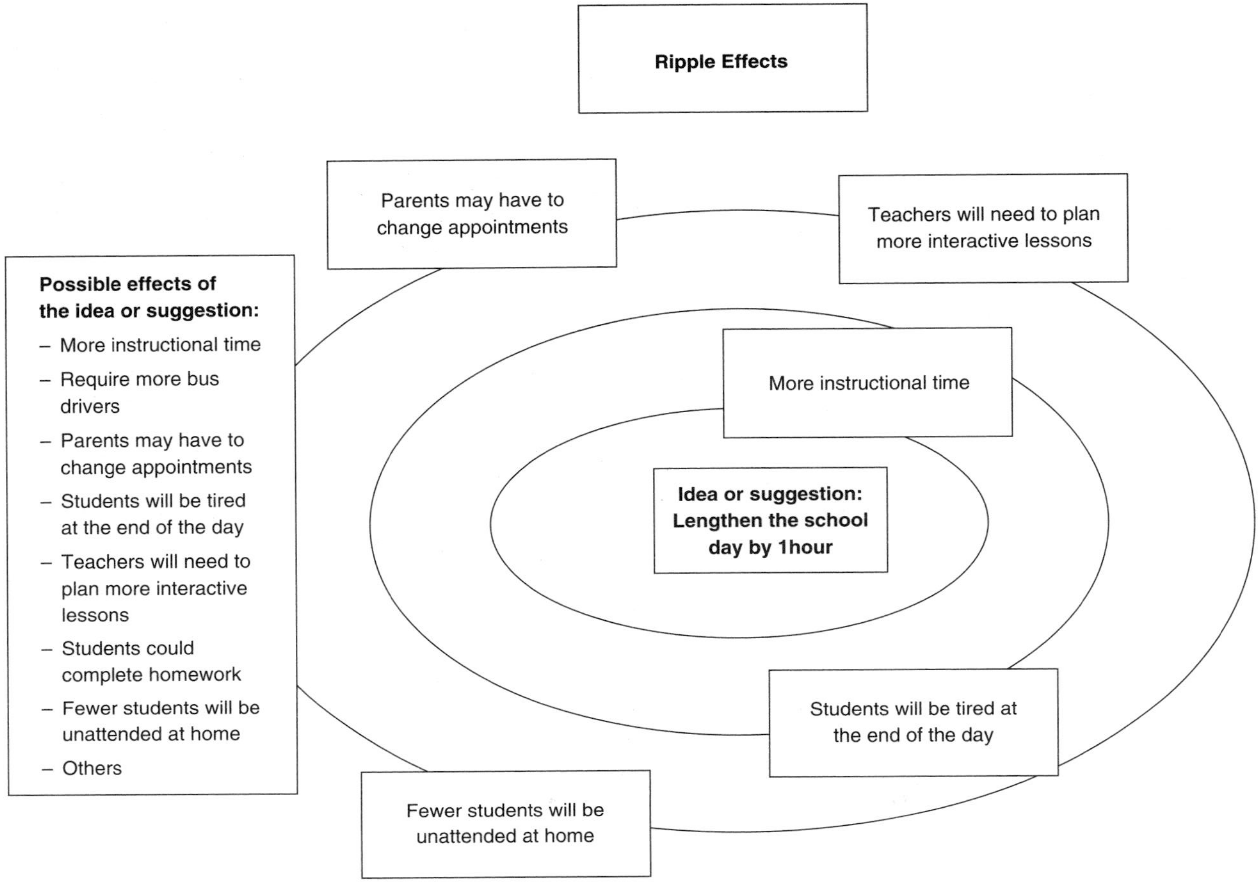

Ripple Effects

Teachers will need to plan more interactive lessons

More instructional time

Idea or suggestion:
Lengthen the school day by 1hour

Students will be tired at the end of the day

Parents may have to change appointments

Fewer students will be unattended at home

Possible effects of the idea or suggestion:
– More instructional time
– Require more bus drivers
– Parents may have to change appointments
– Students will be tired at the end of the day
– Teachers will need to plan more interactive lessons
– Students could complete homework
– Fewer students will be unattended at home
– Others

- Small-Group Multiple Ripple Effects: This variation works in much the same manner as the previous strategy, except that each of the small groups is assigned a different idea or suggestion to analyze. Once all of the groups have completed their small ripple effects charts, they come together to talk about their analysis of the ideas and suggestions. The entire group is involved in making a decision about the implementation of the ideas or suggestions generated and analyzed during this process.
- Sticky Note Ripple Effects: Some groups may not have the inner capacity to work together to identify all of the possible ripple effects of an idea or suggestion. This variation may work well with these kinds of groups. The details of this variation are as follows:

  Each group member is given four to five sticky notes.

  Once the idea or suggestion is listed on the large chart, individuals are given two to three minutes to list as many ripple effects as possible.

  Once the time has expired, the staff members are asked to come up to the chart and place their ripple effects to show their relative impact. All of the individuals can come up at once to place their sticky notes on the chart, or they can take turns.

This is a quick and energizing way to help people to process the impact of their ideas and suggestions.

- Ripple Effects Contest: Often, teachers like to have some type of competition associated with their work. Introducing competition can be fun but one needs to consider the benefits and costs to the collaborative needs of the group members. Assuming that
a little competition will be fun for the group, you may consider offering this variation.

  Divide the larger group into smaller teams of three or four people.

  Give each group a set of colored sticky notes that are a different color than all of the other small groups.

  Post the ripple effects chart on the wall so that all of the group members can see it; explain the idea or suggestion listed on the chart and the directions for the ripple effects contest.

Allow the small groups five minutes to generate as many ripple effects as they can think of and write on their sticky notes.

At the end of the five-minute time limit, ask a representative to post his or her group's sticky notes on the large ripple effects chart at the front of the room; each team earns a point for each unique idea that is posted on the chart. A unique idea means that the idea was not identified by any other group during the process.

The leader posts the scores for each team; the winning team earns some small prize for its efforts.

After the point total has been determined, the entire group talks about the ideas generated and their placement on the ripple effects chart.

Using the information learned in the activity, the group makes a decision regarding the implementation of the idea or suggestion.

- Carousel Ripple Effects: This variation of the basic concept can be fun and energizing for participants. Here are the details:

  Divide the larger group into smaller teams of four or five people.

  Assign each of the smaller teams one idea or suggestion to analyze for ripple effects. Give each of these small teams a chart similar to the one in Figure 4.6.

  Set a time limit of 10 minutes for the first part of the activity. During this time period, the small teams need to talk about their idea or suggestion, make sure they understand it, and generate as many ripple effects related to their assigned idea or suggestion as possible. The ripple effects need to be written on the chart and placed in the ripple that shows their relative impact.

  At the end of the 10-minute development period, ask each small team to designate two traveling members. The rest of the team members will stay at the chart they helped to develop.

  When the leader gives the appropriate signal, the travelers move to the next team and its chart. All of the travelers move in the same direction; the leader designates the movement pattern (could be clockwise or counterclock-wise) at the start of the activity and the amount of time for each "cycle" of the traveling process. (See Figure 4.8 for an illustration of the movement pattern.)

When the travelers reach a new group, their job is to listen to a brief (one-minute) explanation of the original group's work by the original members still at the chart. Once the explanation has been heard, the travelers are required to add two more ripple effects to the chart they are visiting. These new ripple effects need to be written on the chart by the travelers.

Once the time set by the meeting leader for the visitation process has expired, a signal is given and the travelers move to the next group, designated by the movement pattern outlined at the beginning of the process by the group leader.

After three or four visitations, the meeting leader stops the activity and asks the travelers to return to their home groups. The home groups talk about what the travelers and the stayers learned as a result of the activity.

The small teams are asked to share the results of their dialogue with the large group.

The large group makes a decision about the implementation of the ideas or suggestions as a result of the activity.

Opposites Only

Another energizing activity that gets people to think and process information quickly is called Opposites Only. In this energizer, the group members must be constantly thinking as new ideas are generated. Here is a brief summary of how it works with a group:

- The entire group is involved in generating possible ideas or solutions to a problem faced by a school, department, or faculty.
- As each new idea or suggestion is generated, it is listed on a chart at the front of the room.
- After each new idea is listed, the group members are required to think of an idea or suggestion that is the opposite of the one written on the chart. The group leader writes this idea or suggestion next to the original suggestion on the chart. The group is not

Figure 4.8 Sample Movement Pattern

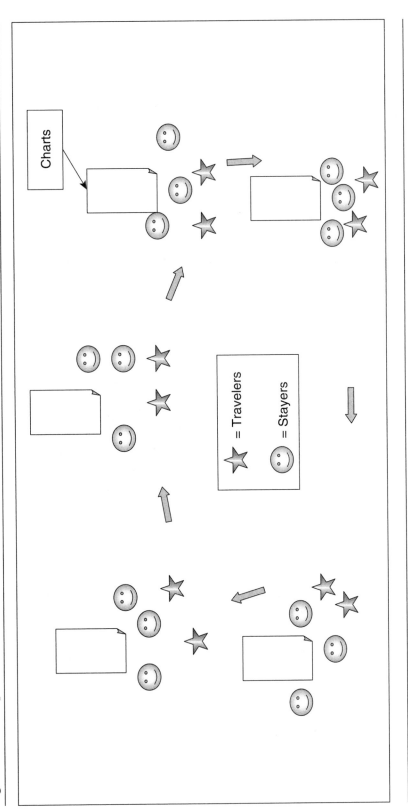

allowed to move forward with any new ideas or suggestions until an opposite is written on the chart.

- The leader asks for a new idea or suggestion, writes it on the chart, and then asks the group members to generate another opposite.
- The process continues until all of the possible ideas or suggestions are exhausted.
- At end of the activity, the entire group talks about the list and makes a decision regarding the implementation of the generated ideas.

Here are some variations that you may consider using when asking your groups to generate opposites:

- Silent Opposites Only: In this variation, group members generate the original idea by talking as a whole group, but they are asked to come up with the opposite silently. Individuals in the group are asked to run up to the chart and write their opposite idea silently. Once an idea is written, the rest of the group verifies that it is truly an opposite by voting with a thumbs-up or thumbs-down signal.
- Team Opposites: Because teachers like to have some level of competition, this variation can appeal to groups. It works like this:

    The larger group is divided into two smaller teams. Each of the teams is issued a noise-making or signaling device such as a bell or horn.

    An original idea or suggestion is placed on a chart at the front of the room.

    Each team can discuss possible opposites; when a team is ready to suggest an opposite, someone in the group sets off the signal.

    The team that sets off its signal first gets to offer its opposite suggestions first; once the suggestion has been given, the opposing team has to agree that the opposite suggestion is truly opposite and that it matches the original idea or suggestion. The leader of the large group is the final judge in cases in which a dispute cannot be resolved.

When a team's opposite idea or suggestion is accepted, that team receives one point.

The game continues until all of the original ideas or suggestions have been assigned an opposite.

The small teams are combined into one large group and asked to talk about the process and to make a decision regarding the implementation of the original ideas and suggestions.

Peeling the Onion

In many instances, the problems that we face have multiple layers or issues that affect the possible solutions a team can generate. In some of these cases, the problem that is most visible to us is the presenting problem or the symptom of a much deeper issue. It is important that teams be able to peel off the surface issues associated with a problem and get to the core of an issue. In Peeling the Onion, teacher teams get an energizing experience in looking beyond the obvious when working through the problems they may face. Here is a brief description of how this activity works with an actual group:

- The leader of the group develops and designs a chart like the one shown in Figure 4.9 to help guide the activity.
- The most obvious or visible part of the issue is written in the area that represents the outer part of the onion.
- The group members are asked to generate a statement that represents an example of something that is occurring behind the scenes or a factor that could be causing the problem on the outer layer of the onion. The generation of the factor could be done as a large group or through discussions in pairs or other small groups. The leader writes down the suggestion on the second layer of the onion.
- The entire group is asked to generate a factor that could be causing the problem or suggestion listed on the second layer of the onion. The leader writes this idea in the third level of the diagram.
- The process is continued until the group exhausts its ideas.
- The leader of the group asks the members to talk about what they learned as a result of the activity and to make a decision regarding a solution to the original problem written on the top level of the onion diagram.

Figure 4.9   Peeling the Onion Chart

Peeling the Onion

Layer 1 Presenting problem

_____

_____

_____

Layer 2 Deeper level affecting the presenting problem

_____

_____

_____

Layer 3 Deeper level affecting Layer 2 situation

_____

_____

_____

Layer 4 Deeper level affecting Layer 3 situation

_____

_____

_____

_____

Assessing the Impact of Your Engagement Efforts

In most cases, the change in your staff meetings that occurs as a result of implementing energizing activities will be obvious. You'll notice that your teachers are more interested in working together, they are better able to solve problems, and meetings are more fun and engaging. Beyond these obvious changes, your staff may be making growth in other, more significant ways. As a teacher, it is important for you to assess the impact of these changes and make sure that your staff is aware of their growth as a group. In this section, we'll explore some options that are both simple to implement and informative.

Group Norms

Effective, productive groups exhibit certain predictable behaviors. In group work, we call these behaviors *norms*. The word "norm" refers to a normal or regular behavior used by a group. In his book *Effective Group Facilitation in Education* (2004), John discusses the concept of norms and their impact on group effectiveness. Even though there are many norms that a productive group may exhibit, there are several that align closely with the use of energizing activities.

- Idea consideration: The group puts a lot of ideas on the table before choosing the final selections for consideration.
- Understanding suggestion: Team members seek to gain clarification about suggestions before judging whether they are appropriate to the problem.
- Collaboration: Teachers are able to work in a variety of groupings with little difficulty.
- Integration: Team members use information from a variety of sources in making decisions.
- Clear processes: The team members use established and overt processes for making decisions and operating the team.
- Conflict resolution: Team members are able to disagree about issues during the decision-making process and use conflict as a productive source of energy.
- Perspective: Teachers see problem solving and decision making as fun and productive. They are able to see other perspectives and the potential impact of their decisions on others in the school community.

Effective groups develop and follow many other norms as they work together to make decisions. We have found that the ones mentioned here are the foundation of group success. As you work with your teams, ask them to identify norms that will help them to succeed as they work together. Your teams can adopt and use these norms to become even more successful in their work together.

Strategies for Helping a Group to Assess Its Progress

Group Debriefing

At the end of a meeting in which energizing activities have been implemented, the group leader can hold a debriefing of the session. These group debriefings can be done in two or three minutes but allow the group itself to see its accomplishments. Normally, leaders pick one or two norms and ask the group members to share their perceptions of the meeting in relation to the selected norms. See how Sharon used a debriefing with a group of teachers in the following example:

At the end of a meeting about progress on the school improvement plan, Sharon took a few minutes and asked the team members to reflect on their progress as a group. She posted two questions on chart paper:

A. How did we do today in getting clarification about suggestions before we made our final selection?
B. How enjoyable was it to work together as a team?

She asked everyone to read the questions and think about the answers for 20 to 30 seconds. Next, she had the group members meet in pairs to talk about their perceptions of their progress on the two norms. Finally, she held an open discussion on the two questions. Most people who responded said they thought that the group had done a good job with getting clarification before making their decisions, but they still didn't think the meetings were as enjoyable as they could be. Sharon asked the group members to talk in pairs about how the team could overcome this problem. After a brief discussion, they came up with two or three suggestions for making their meetings more enjoyable. Sharon decided to try these suggestions out at the next meeting.

Sharon's actions in this example might sound very simple, but they were highly effective. Her strategy matched the group's need for energy and interaction. By having people work in pairs before talking as a large group, she modeled an energizing activity. Sharon also helped the group members see how they were doing by holding the discussion as a whole group. Another thing that Sharon accomplished by holding small-group and then large-group discussions was that she communicated that team members *should* be making growth in the norm areas of the discussion. These subtle messages are powerful in their communication to the group. When leaders hold debriefing exercises, such as the one Sharon held in this example, on a regular basis, group members begin to *believe* they need to grow in the areas addressed by the leader. This subtle but powerful message is communicated by the leader and his or her actions.

Observational Checklists

Another strategy employed by leaders to assess team member growth is the use of an observational checklist. In using an observational checklist, the leader determines several focus areas in advance of the meeting then watches for them during the course of the meeting. A sample observational checklist is included in Figure 4.10.

Figure 4.10　Sample Observational Checklist

Group Behavior	Occurrences	Effectiveness		
		L	M	E
Group uses appropriate pauses before commenting on suggestions.				
People are engaged in activities.				
Teachers mix in groups other than core teaching groups.				
Staff members follow the process of activities.				
People get started on activities within one minute of receiving directions.				

Directions: Use the checklist to observe effective meeting behaviors during a staff meeting. Mark down the number of times a behavior is observed in the Occurrences column; after the meeting, rate the group on its meeting behavior using the L, M, and E columns. In this checklist, L = Limited level of skill expertise; M = Moderate level of skill expertise; E = Excellent level of skill expertise. Feel free to add in the specific skills that you are assessing in your staff meeting.

At selected times during the meeting, the leader actually uses the checklist to look for evidence of team effectiveness. At the end of the meeting, the leader could share the information gathered on the checklist with the staff members.

Instead of the leader observing the group members as they work, a process observer from the large group could be chosen. This person would not be engaged in the meeting but would be assigned to observe group processing in two or three areas and to provide feedback at the end of the meeting.

In another variation, observers could be selected to complete an observational checklist within small work teams if they are used during the meeting. In this case, several people would need to report on the group's effectiveness during the meeting.

We're This Good

In this energizing debriefing strategy, the entire group is involved in simultaneously giving feedback about the meeting. It works like this:

- At the end of the meeting, the leader writes or verbally shares questions or prompts that are related to the group's progress on predetermined norms. The following are examples of these ideas:

    How did we do today in getting lots of ideas on the chart before we started to consider each idea?

    How did we do today in considering multiple perspectives in making our decisions?

    How did we do today in working together in small groups?

    How did we do today in sticking to our established processes?

- As each question or prompt is shared, the leader asks group members to signal the relative effectiveness of the group. The signaling involves group members holding their hands like fishermen do when they describe their most recent catch; the hands should be held close together for low effectiveness, far apart for high effectiveness. All of the group members should vote simultaneously. The group leader should ask them to look at the signals of the others. By looking at the other signals, they will get an idea of how others see the group.

Classroom Observation

Another informal measure that can give the leader an indication of the effectiveness of meetings is to look for the use of energizing activities in the teachers' classrooms. If you are doing a good job providing an energizing and engaging atmosphere in your staff meetings, several of your teachers will find ideas they would like to try in their classrooms. As you do informal, walk-through visits, look for activities from your meetings to pop up in your teachers' classrooms. At this point in the process, it is important to keep these observations informal and not a part of the performance-appraisal process. As you see examples of your meeting energizers in action in classrooms, be sure to let teachers know that you noticed. Also, it might be a good idea to keep a log or journal of the energizing activities that you see in the classrooms. A log can help you to see which energizers are most meaningful to your teachers. You may want to use these on a more regular basis in your staff meetings because they are motivating to your teachers.

Gauge Our Growth

In this energizing feedback mechanism, the leader gets information from participants in a fun and interesting manner. The activity works like this:

- At the end of the meeting, the leader verbally poses questions or prompts to the group members regarding their perceptions of the meeting and the group norms associated with the energizers used in the meeting. The teachers signal their level of agreement through the use of a small gauge or meter they have been provided with at the beginning of the meeting. Some examples of questions or prompts that could be asked of teachers include the following:

  Using the gauges I have provided, rate us as a group in our ability to work together.

  How did we do with regard to brainstorming lots of ideas before settling on two or three for final consideration?

  How well did we take into account all of the perspectives affected by this decision in our planning and discussions?

- After each question or prompt is given, each teacher uses the gauge to signal his or her relative rating of the component being assessed. For instructions on how to make the gauge, see Figure 4.11.
- As all of the gauges are shown, the meeting leader does a quick scan of the group and reports the relative scores.
- At the end of the activity, the group can discuss what it learned about its progress and what it wants to do.

Your gauge should look like the illustration in Figure 4.11.

Figure 4.11   Feedback Gauge

- Draw a gauge on card stock. An index card will work for most applications.
- Make a pointer out of a piece of black paper.
- Fasten the pointer to the gauge with a brass brad.
- Laminate the gauge parts if you want them to last several years.

Surveys and Questionnaires

Sometimes, leaders want more comprehensive growth information about their group than the simple strategies illustrated previously can give. In these instances, you may consider using surveys and questionnaires with your group. Although there are many possible surveys that you could use with your group, we have chosen to focus on a couple in this book. These two were selected because of their ease of implementation and analysis. We know that many of you and your teachers have limited time, so it's important that your instruments be easy to implement and analyze.

These types of instruments should work well for you because you're probably looking for general information from your group to guide you in your implementation of energizing activities.

Scaled Feedback

With these kinds of instruments, staff members are asked to respond to a predetermined survey to get their general thoughts about the group's progress related to the implementation of energizing activities. Some leaders want to determine the degree to which a group is growing. Example A provides a rating card on which participants have a chance to actually rate the degree to which growth has occurred. Other leaders are satisfied just knowing that some growth has occurred in a group; Example B provides participants a chance to provide feedback on whether a skill is present in the group.

Example A	Example B

Group-Processing Skill Assessment	
Our group generates lots of ideas to consider.	1 2 3 4 5
We are able to see other people's perspectives in relation to the ideas generated.	1 2 3 4 5
Our team is able to work through conflict in a productive manner.	1 2 3 4 5
We work well together in making decisions.	1 2 3 4 5

Group-Processing Skill Assessment		
Our group generates lots of ideas to consider.	Yes	No
We are able to see other people's perspectives in relation to the ideas generated.	Yes	No
Our team is able to work through conflict in a productive manner.	Yes	No
We work well together in making decisions.	Yes	No

In both of these examples, the leader administering them has a chance to quickly determine whether a skill is present in the group in a quick and easy manner.

Group Surveys

Although there are many ways to survey a group, we will focus on one in this section, the open-ended response. In this type of survey, each respondent is given a small number of questions or prompts and asked to respond to these through written comments. Open-ended responses allow a leader to gather data in the form of narrative responses. Open-ended response surveys allow a wider set of information to be gathered by the leader. An example of an open-ended response survey follows in Figure 4.12.

Figure 4.12 Open-Ended Response Survey

Group Effectiveness Survey

Please respond the following questions and prompts about how our group works together. Your responses will be used to plan our future meetings.

1. How do you think we work together as a team to make decisions? Share examples that illustrate your major points.

2. Describe how our group handles conflict.

3. What energizing strategies have we implemented that have helped our team to improve our relationships? Why do you think this has worked in the way that it has with our group?

Teacher-Conducted Feedback Sessions

We have found that this format for data gathering has produced positive results over the years. Teachers are normally more open with their peers than the leader, who is their boss.

In setting up a teacher-conducted feedback session, it is important to keep the following ideas in mind:

- Be sure that the teachers you pick feel confident in leading a discussion involving their peers.
- Frame the role of the teachers leading the feedback session; as you introduce the session, let the rest of the teachers know that you have asked the teachers facilitating the session to gather information about the rest of the staff's feelings about the energized staff meetings.
- Provide the questions and prompts that the facilitators will use to get feedback from the rest of the teachers. See an example in Figure 4.13.
- Thank both the teachers who facilitated the meeting and the rest of the staff for sharing their opinions. Let them know how much you appreciate the information you are getting.

Summary

Now that you have completed this chapter, you have a repertoire of techniques to help you maintain the focus and involvement of staff members who are involved in the meetings that you operate. The wide variety of

Figure 4.13   Facilitation Guide

As you facilitate the discussion of our meeting effectiveness, be sure to get information on the following:

1. The overall impact of our energizing efforts

2. How the group feels that we work through conflict

3. The group's rating on our level of collaboration. Specific examples of times we have collaborated well.

4. How we do in using other stakeholder perspectives when making decisions.

activities and strategies presented here will benefit you and your staff members as you work together as a team. When people are fully engaged in a meeting, they are able to share their ideas and help with problem-solving opportunities. This maximizes the human resources at your disposal and builds a sense of efficacy among those you lead.

In this chapter, we also looked at ways to find out how your meeting-improvement efforts are working. It's important to find out how things are going for your staff and what areas they see as needing additional work. From our experience, we have found that informal, regular feedback methods can be very helpful in keeping your meeting-improvement efforts on track and focused. As you lead meetings, be sure to look for evidence that you are keeping everyone engaged and involved. Watching for this evidence also can inform you about the fruits of your efforts to improve your meetings.

As an informal assessment for your own learning, take a few minutes to ask yourself the following questions:

- What did I learn from this chapter that will help me to make my meetings more engaging and energizing?
- What activities did I learn about in this chapter that might help my staff to work together?
- How can I informally assess the effectiveness of my meetings with staff?

In Chapter 5, we will examine strategies and ideas to help your staff become more emotionally connected with and invested in each other. These connections will help them as they learn how to work together and experience the conflict and chaos that can sometimes enter into team relationships. You will find this information helpful as you move your team into the next phase of its operation.

5

Building on the Positive Emotional Connections of Staff Members

*Treat people as if they were what they ought to be, and you help
them to become what they are capable of being.*

—Johann Wolfgang von Goethe

Human behavior is guided by emotions. This principle can help
you as you work to energize your staff meetings and bring out
the best in your employees. Beyond just energizing and firing up the
people you lead, you can connect to their emotions as you work to
solve problems and increase productivity. This use of emotional connections actually helps your group members as they work together
and increases their effectiveness as a group and as individuals. In this
chapter, you will learn the following:

- The importance of emotional connections
- Techniques and strategies to use emotional connections to help a group build on positive experiences
- Ideas to help you disconnect negative thought patterns and replace them with positive ones
- Methods to help you decide whether using emotional connections is appropriate and how much emotion to access

The Importance of Emotional Connections

It is crucial to work with your staff members to help them build positive professional connections with each other. Even though people may resist the building of relationships, they need to go beyond casual conversation if they are to work together in a collaborative manner. The positive connections you build now will come in handy when your group encounters conflict and chaos as they begin to attack the issues that affect the core mission of the school.

Techniques and Strategies to Use Emotional Connections to Build on Positive Experiences

Block of Support

A positive way to begin a meeting is to provide each staff member with a two-inch wooden cube. Have each staff member write his or her name on the block and pass it to the person on the right. That person then writes a positive word or phrase on the block. Continue passing the blocks around the room until all sides of the blocks are filled. If some staff members are not at the meeting during this activity, make sure to start a block for them. After the block has been passed around the room, the owner gets it back. This person now has a block with at least six positive comments on it. In our experience, teachers often keep these blocks in prominent spots on their desks for years. At times, we have even asked people to bring their blocks to a meeting to remind them of the activity. Some teachers have used this idea in their classrooms with students.

Bag of Positive Phrases

At the beginning of the meeting, give each staff member a bag or sack. Have the staff member decorate the bag and put his or her name on the bag. Place the bags at locations around the room. Provide each person at the meeting with some sticky notes or other note paper, and have staff members write positive notes to one another, placing the notes in the bags around the room. The staff members can either sign their names or they can be anonymous. After 5–10 minutes, stop the writing part of the activity and have the owners of the bags pick up their sacks. Give them a minute or two to read the notes they received. Ask staff members to think about what they learned as they wrote the notes and as they read the notes that others wrote about them.

This is a rewarding activity for the staff to do. It is exciting to watch the staff read their notes. This activity would be fun to do during February, when people can get bogged down and need something to lift their spirits. If you don't have time during a faculty meeting, you can place the bags around the room in the faculty lounge, and give people a set amount of time to write their notes. The "full" bags can be brought to a faculty meeting or placed in faculty members' mailboxes. It is important to include all staff members, such as cooks, custodians, office staff, teachers, and paraprofessionals in this activity. Even though it is a simple idea, it builds a strong, positive atmosphere among the school faculty. We have seen staff members who have kept their "bag of positives" close to their desk or workstation for a number of years after completing the activity.

Spread the Word

For this strategy, you will need markers and a flat bedsheet, tablecloth, or large piece of paper. On a long table or large wall surface, spread out the cloth or paper, and tell staff members that you will give them 5–10 minutes to write down as many positive comments as they can think of about each other. Ask each staff member to write down a certain number of comments or to write comments about certain people (to make sure that everyone has at least one comment on the chart). As you lead the activity, be sure to look at the chart or cloth as people are writing to make sure that everyone is receiving a positive comment. If you notice that someone is not getting comments, stop and write something about him or her. This is another activity that works well posted in the staff lounge over a set period of time. This gives people a chance to think and write down many comments. Use several sheets divided by grade level or department if you are working with a large faculty.

Once a large number of comments have been written down, display the completed chart or sheet in the lounge or in a place where the staff gathers. At follow-up staff meetings, ask people what they learned about the activity and how they think it helped them to connect and work together. Also, ask people how this activity could be helpful in their work with students.

Ideas to Help You Disconnect Negative Thought Patterns and Replace Them With Positive Ones

Blossoming With Positive Goals

In your lounge, make a large tree out of paper. On colored leaves, write all of the positive things that are occurring at your building. You also could celebrate the goals that you have reached as a building by putting each goal on a leaf and placing it on the tree.

The goals that your building is working on can be placed at the bottom of the tree to show that they are in progress. It is important that your goals be specific and clear so that they can be observed in action. This strategy helps people to see the progress they have made and what is left to accomplish. It provides a visual aid to help people to see what has been completed. We have found that staff members look forward to seeing another leaf placed on the tree. At times, we have placed the leaves on the tree during staff meetings and used the event as a reason for celebration. We have even asked staff members who were key to the accomplishment of a goal to place the leaf on the tree.

For some staff members, a tree may not hold a lot of meaning. For these people, you might consider something else that has meaning for them, such as a plant with flowers, a tower, a house foundation, a pathway, or another visual aid. Even though this type of activity sounds simple, it brings meaning and positive emotions to the goal-accomplishment process. It can pay big dividends with a staff. It can help them to overcome the perception that goal attainment is boring and just a lot of work, and it allows them to have fun and celebrate their accomplishments. It can be used at the classroom level to motivate students and at the adult level to motivate staff members.

Reward With a Smile

Another way of providing staff with a positive reinforcement is to fill a container with treats, such as M&M's candy, jelly beans, candy bars, etc. For example, I was able to find a container that had a smiley face on the lid of the container, and I provided a positive note to the staff member explaining why they were receiving the treat. The staff member who receives the container eats the candy, enjoys the note, and then fills it with candy, adds a positive note, and passes it on to another staff member. This strategy helps to build emotional connections because the person receiving the note does not expect it and suddenly gets it in his or her mailbox. We have seen people look in their mailbox and let out a loud "alright!" when they pulled out the candy box. The excitement of this activity goes beyond the candy; it relates to the fact that someone on the staff cared enough about them to think about them, write a note, and pass on the container.

This activity works well when there are several containers circulating among the faculty at once. We have found that it works well when we start the candy containers at the same time and post time limits on their passing. Normally, it works well to have the containers change hands about once a week. You can remind staff members to pass the containers in the weekly bulletin or though some other method. We have tried to watch the process to make sure that the containers kept moving and added more containers when we noticed holdups.

Be sure to talk about the activity in staff meetings to get people's perceptions of what they are gaining as a result of passing the containers. After a period of time (maybe a month or two), it is a good idea to call in the containers and give people a break from the activity. You want to keep the activity from becoming stale and overused. In the future, you may want to vary the reward (coupons, sticker pages, or other rewards). Be sure to include everyone on your staff in the activity, such as custodians, cooks, paraprofessionals, secretaries, the principal, and others who could benefit from receiving positive feedback about their performance or personality at school.

A Novel Staff

This activity can be fun and helps people to connect in a positive manner. It involves having the group compile a book about the staff. The basic strategy works like this:

- Purchase a blank book at a local bookstore.
- Designate a page for each staff member; write his or her name on the page. Circulate the book among the staff and ask people to write positive comments, stories, or other interesting anecdotes about the person. Provide enough time for people to think and fill in the book. It may take several staff meetings or a couple of weeks to accomplish this.

- Once the book is completed, place it where the staff members have access to it and can look it at from time to time.

This activity has several variations that you might want to consider to make it even more engaging for your staff.

- Ask staff members to make their pages more personal by writing some information about themselves, such as their background, educational philosophy, thoughts about teaching, etc. This helps others to learn something about each staff member as they write positive statements about each person.
- Have individuals put together a collage or drawing that illustrates themselves as a person and a professional. This illustration can be created on another piece of paper and pasted into the book.
- Ask staff members to select their favorite poem, phrase, or quotation to include as an example of their beliefs. Staff members will learn something about their colleagues as they write compliments or positive ideas.
- Have team members or colleagues develop illustrations, poems, quotations, or other writings that represent each person as a person and a professional. This will also help staff members to learn how others view them.

Floating or Traveling Trophy

There are several ways a staff could use a floating or traveling trophy. Here are some you might consider:

- For the staff member who did or said the funniest or most humorous thing at school
- For the person who made the biggest funny mistake
- For the teacher who turned around a difficult student
- For the person who helped out other staff members with a problem
- For the teacher who had the most interesting parent–teacher conference story
- For any other reason that would be entertaining or meaningful for staff

To do this, you might find an old trophy and put your own label or title on it. You could use a statue in place of a trophy, such as a flamingo, cow, lion, or some other interesting figurine. This simple idea can become meaningful for staff members over the years. People look forward to the presentation of the trophy and nominate others for funny and meaningful awards. The traveling trophies are very motivational for people and builds a positive culture in the school.

Snowball Fight

The snowball fight activity can be an energizing and emotional building experience for your staff members. It also helps people get to know each other in a deeper and more meaningful way than they normally do in a staff setting. Here is how it works:

- Each teacher is given a blank sheet of paper.
- The meeting leader asks each teacher to write the following on his or her paper:

    Share something about yourself that nobody in the room knows.

    If you could have one wish come true, what would it be?

    Share a significant moment that touched your life as a teacher.

    Draw a rough picture of a place that makes you feel happy and relaxed.

- The whole group is divided into two equal groups that stand in two single-file lines facing each other; individuals crumple their papers into a paper wad or snowball.
- At the leader's signal, the groups throw their paper wads at each other as if they were having a snowball fight.
- Group members pick up the "snowballs" that land by them and throw them at others; they continue to keep the fight going until the leader calls time.
- Everyone picks up a paper wad, unravels it, and tries to find the person in the room to whom it belongs. Once they locate that person, they engage in conversation about the information on the paper. This part of the process can be a little chaotic as people try to find the "owners" of the paper wads, but it usually works itself out in a few minutes.
- Team members continue to move around the room until all of the paper owners are located and a discussion is held. This may take several pairings.

- Once everyone has been identified, the entire group engages in a conversation. You may have the group discuss questions such as the following:

  What did you learn from this activity?

  How do you feel that learning more about each other will help us as we work together in the future?

  What clues did you use to find the person who matched your picture?

  How might this activity be used in a classroom?

The Rest of the Story

An emotional connection can be built by helping two people to work together on an imaginary situation. The "rest of the story" can provide an emotional tie by helping teams of teachers to generate positive closure to situations. It works like this:

- Divide the larger group into pairs. Make sure that the people who are paired do not work together on a regular basis.
- Ask one member of each pair to be designated as Person A, the other as Person B.
- Provide each pair with a half-sheet of paper.
- Ask Person A to write down a real problem that he or she has faced during the last month. The problem must be describable in one or two sentences. Person A should write down only the problem, not the solution.
- The paper is given to Person B. He or she reads the problem and finishes the story with a solution to the problem. Person B needs to be as detailed as possible in providing a solution to Person A. The solution should be written in a positive manner.
- Have Persons A and B talk about the process they experienced and what they learned as a result of the activity.
- Have the pairs form teams of four and have the members talk about the process, the problems, and the solutions generated and what they learned about each other as a result of the activity.

This activity can be used in a variety of ways to help teachers learn more about each other and to see there may be more than meets the eye in the situations they see and experience in their work with children. Here are some of the most common ideas we have seen in our work with schools as they have implemented this activity:

- Have Person A generate a real problem, but have Person B generate one or two reasons why this problem could be presenting itself in the school or classroom. This activity helps teachers to see the reasons behind some of the issues that they face.
- Ask Person A to generate a problem, and then have Person B describe the impact of the problem from a predetermined stakeholder's perspective. For example, if Person A described a problem with homework completion, Person B would need to describe the impact of homework difficulties from the student's perspective. This variation helps teachers to see another person's perspective.
- Ask Person A to briefly describe a situation he or she faced recently and how the problem was solved. Person B reads this description and generates a statement that describes the ripple effects of the solution that Person A came up with. This activity helps people to see the effects of their decisions.

Visioning the Solution

This simple but effective strategy can help a team to see how it will solve a problem. It can be used with a variety of problem-generation techniques. In this description, we will focus on using this strategy to help teachers to think about the ideas they have generated and the effects of their decisions. Here is a general description of how the strategy is implemented:

- A list of possible solutions is generated by the group. The group may use brainstorming or other techniques to generate a list of possible solutions to a problem or situation that the group faces.
- The group leader chooses one of the possible solutions and reads it to the group.
- The leader asks the teachers at the meeting to visualize how the school would look if the solution were implemented; some groups may benefit from being asked to close their eyes. Some of the questions or prompts that leaders have found helpful in working with their teachers on this process include the following:

> Close your eyes. How would our school look if this idea were fully implemented?

> As you think about this implementation, what would the school look like, feel like, and sound like if this idea were implemented successfully?

Take a minute and close your eyes. Imagine it is one year from now. Visualize how our school would be different as a result of this idea and our work as a team.

In your mind, step back from the school and look in as an outsider. What differences do you see as a result of this idea being implemented; be sure to see both the pros and the cons.

- After about 30 seconds or so, the leader asks the teachers to form small groups of three or four and talk about their visions.
- After individuals have shared, each group is asked to put together a collective vision that can be shared with the larger group.
- This process is repeated until all of the possible ideas have been considered; the large group is asked to select the best idea based on what they saw during the visualization process.
- At the end of the exercise, the group is asked to consider the following questions:

What did you learn as a result of the visualization activity?

How did this process help you to narrow your choices? What were some of the difficulties that you found in using this process?

How could the idea of visualizing solutions be used in a classroom with students?

The Other Perspectives

Many times, our staff members get so tied up in their own situations that they have a hard time seeing other people's perspectives. This activity helps teachers purposefully look at problems and solutions from the perspective of others who are affected by the decisions that they make. Here are the major steps in the process:

- The group is asked to brainstorm a list of all of the stakeholders that could be affected by the decisions the group is attempting to study.
- Divide the larger team into smaller teams representing each of the stakeholder groups generated in the brainstorming session.
- Give each of the smaller teams five minutes to examine the potential decision from the perspective of the stakeholder group they are representing. Have each team write down the major

points that their stakeholder group needs to have considered in a discussion about the ideas or solutions.

- At the end of the planning time, bring all of the stakeholder team representatives back together. Have the entire group engage in a discussion about the ideas or solutions to the problem. In the discussion, all of the stakeholder perspectives must be brought up and addressed.

- After the discussion, ask the entire group to make a decision about the implementation of the ideas or solutions. Have the large group talk about what they learned as a result of the activity and what they learned about each other in the process. Have them consider how this activity could be implemented in classrooms.

Construction of the Problem

Often, a visual representation of a solution or a problem will engage people's minds in generating innovative and powerful ideas. This activity gets people's creative juices flowing and helps to turn on some very powerful problem-solving strategies. It is not only visual in nature but also fun and difficult at the same time. We have gotten great results in situations in which the norm would have been to generate some pretty basic and predictable responses to unusual problems. Here are the basic steps of the strategy:

- Divide the larger group up into smaller problem-solving teams.
- Assign each team to solve the entire problem or a portion of the larger problem.
- Tell the small teams that they will need to talk about their ideas in their group then put together a construction or sculpture that represents their proposed solution to the problem.
- Provide a box of materials for the small groups to use in their constructions. You may consider placing the following materials in the box:

Construction paper

Pipe cleaners

Paper clips

Glue

Feathers

Buttons

Small boxes

Aluminum foil

Wire

Sequins

Small strips of wood

Markers

Paint

Paper towel rolls

Other items as the leader finds appropriate

- Provide the teams with ample time to complete the projects. We have found that this process takes longer than just having the teams engage in discussions. Usually 20–25 minutes gives teams a chance to think and build a quality sculpture.
- As the teams are working, walk around and monitor their progress. Add more time for completion if needed.
- When all of the teams have finished or are near completion, let them know about the procedures for presenting their projects. These are usually fairly simple but need to be given at this point because most of the group's energy has been used up in the building process. The major points to consider for the presentations are the following:

Each team will have two to three minutes to share its sculpture and explain its significance.

Each team member needs to be meaningfully involved in the presentation.

The team doing the presentation needs to clearly show how its sculpture illustrates the potential solution.

A period at the end of the presentation needs to be set aside for group comments and questions.

- Give each team a short amount of time to share its construction. Have all of the teams comment about what they learned about each other and the problem as a result of the activity.

Meaningful Presentations

Meaningful presentations have some relationship to the construction idea just presented. They also get people's emotions more engaged in looking at potential solutions to a problem and can be used to help people to summarize their understanding of the meeting content or concepts. We have seen people really have fun with this idea and gain some meaningful learning in the process. Here are the steps we use to implement it in groups:

- Divide the larger group into smaller teams of five to six people.
- Tell them that they will be working together as a team to clarify the ideas or potential solutions to a problem facing the group. After they have had a chance to talk about and clarify their understanding of the situation, it is their job to put together a meaningful presentation that best represents their understanding of the idea or solution.
- Let the group know that what they do in their meaningful presentations is up to them. They need to provide information that will be meaningful to them and to others in the large group. They might do a skit, develop a song, design a chant, put together a poster, build a sculpture, or do whatever they want to clearly communicate a basic understanding of the idea or topic.
- Give the group ample time to complete their meaningful presentations. Usually, we give groups between 30 and 45 minutes depending on the complexity of the content. Allow the groups to work outside the normal meeting room so that they have privacy in putting together their meaningful presentations.
- At the end of the work time, bring all of the groups back together and give each small group three to five minutes to share its meaningful presentation. At the end of their presentation, the team needs to find a way to assess the learning of the other large-group members.
- Hold a discussion with the entire group after all of the small-group presentations. Here is a sample of some of the questions that you may ask them to debrief the activity:

> What did you learn about the topics as a result of the presentations?
>
> What did you learn about each other in the process?
>
> How do you see this activity working in a classroom? What problems might need to be addressed for the students to have success?

Climate Check

In energized staff meetings, it is important to keep an eye on the emotional climate. People can become so engaged in the activities

Figure 5.1   Climate Check Meter

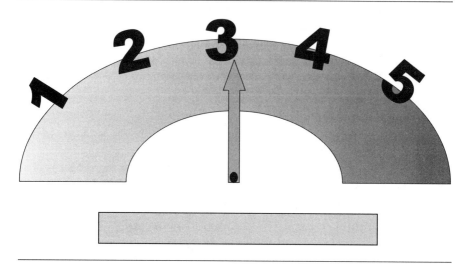

that it is easy for them to forget about their relationships with each other. We have used an idea called a "climate check" to gauge the short-term emotional health of a group. It works like this:

- Construct emotional gauges similar to the one depicted in Figure 5.1.
- Pass out the gauges to the staff at the beginning of the meeting.
- Periodically throughout the meeting, stop and ask the teachers to do a climate check.
- Ask them to respond on a scale from 1 to 5, with 5 being the highest and 1 being the lowest on a scale of positive feelings; you also might ask them to respond in reverse, looking at emotional interference.
- Talk about the results of the climate check as a large group. Involve the entire team in figuring out what to do about the results of the climate check.

Boot Award

The objective of the Boot Award is to reward staff members for something positive they did for another employee or for students. Any staff member can nominate someone for the Boot Award. A sample nomination form is included in Figure 5.2.

Figure 5.2   Boot Award Nomination

I nominate _____ for the Boot Award because he or she helped
me with a science project.

Signature _____

The Boot Award is a way of rewarding staff and providing them with an opportunity during the day to visit classrooms, do some research, finish a project, or anything of their choice. When an employee receives the Boot Award, the principal covers the person's job for a specified period of time. You can provide the employee with as much time as you choose. We have found that covering a staff member's job for one to two hours is practical and makes the award worthwhile for the employee. The nomination box for the Boot Award can be placed in the lounge or the office so that people have easy access to it.

Baggage

If you are working with a staff that has difficulty getting along with each other, this activity can help them deal with their issues. People need to find a way to get their problems behind them. This activity has been successful in helping teachers to get rid of their baggage. Here are the steps you should follow:

- Begin by telling the staff members that you are aware there are many issues that need to be dealt with before they can work together.
- Have people write down the issues that are bothering them. You can have the staff share the issues or just write them down. It is important for staff to have a written copy of their concerns so that they can "place" them later in the activity.
- Let the staff members know that once they have written down the issues, they will be placed in a suitcase, which then will be locked. The team members need to agree that once the issues are locked in the suitcase, they cannot be taken out and used against each other or discussed.
- The leader encourages the staff members to talk about any issues they feel need to be addressed before the suitcase is

closed. This is their chance to resolve the issues before they are off limits for discussion.

- Before the suitcase is closed, the leader needs to get a verbal commitment from each staff member that all of the issues in the suitcase need to remain in the suitcase.
- The leader closes the suitcase and locks it to show that it can't be opened again.

We have found that getting rid of baggage can be a difficult task for teachers. You may find that even though the suitcase has been locked and people have agreed to leave their baggage inside, some people will violate the rules of this activity. You will need to be firm in your interactions at times to make sure that the issues locked in the suitcase don't get out. Verbally remind staff of their agreement to help them work past the temptation to bring up old issues. If you can help the group to work through the initial stages of the "baggage release" process, you will find they can let go of old problems and work toward a positive future.

Positively Hanging

We can't do enough to reinforce the positive aspects of the team members in our schools. This activity helps team members recognize the positive attributes of other team members, but it also helps people to see the good points they have to offer others in their school. It works like this:

- The leader provides supplies for the staff members to use in constructing mobiles. Some of the most common supplies we have provided when we have used this activity with teachers are clothes hangers, paper, paper clips, string, and markers.
- Each staff member is given a piece of paper and a hanger and asked to write his or her name on the piece of paper and attach it to the hanger.
- Once this step has been completed, the staff member passes his or her hanger to the next person.
- The person receiving the hanger writes a positive note about the other staff member and attaches it to the hanger. The staff member can make the note any shape he or she wants before attaching it to the hanger.
- The hangers are passed around until there are at least five to seven positive notes on the hanger.

- The originator of the hanger gets it back once all of the "notes" have been attached; he or she gets a chance to read it.
- The staff member can take the mobile back to the classroom and hang it up.

School Mascot

Another item that you could use to reward staff is a school mascot that can be passed around the building. A small model, drawing, or stuffed animal representing the school mascot can be given to a staff member, classroom, group of students, or individual student in recognition of something positive they have done for the school. This can be done at a public event at which most of the school community is gathered.

Another way to bring the school together is to have a schoolwide meeting. Sheila calls hers "Fabulous Fridays." At these meetings, in addition to the mascot award, she has students sing the school song and invites staff members to talk about the positive things that are going on at the school. This is a good time for the school community to talk about and set some building-wide goals for the school to work on. She shares these ideas with the student body or involves teachers in sharing them. By sharing goals with students on a regular basis, they understand what her group is working on as a building. It is a wonderful way to get everyone together to celebrate all of the positive things happening at the school. It also shows that it takes everyone working together to meet the goals.

The person or group who receives the award keeps the mascot until the next meeting. At the next meeting, that person or class awards it to another person who has been nominated to receive it. This helps to establish a ritual that keeps positive thoughts and ideas in front of the staff and students as they work together to improve the school.

Summary and Next Steps

Emotions are an important factor to consider in planning energizing meetings. It may be difficult to determine how to connect people to emotional experiences and which strategies for using emotional ideas will help a group to be more productive. You need to consider how your staff might respond to positive emotional activities and how you can help them get over their initial discomfort and resistance to new ideas. If you can stay the course, you will find that your efforts will be rewarded by a group of people who are more engaged, positive, invested in the school and others, and better able to focus on the success of the students.

In this chapter, you learned the importance of emotional experiences and strategies for using them in meetings. As you work with groups, take note of how these ideas work and what challenges you face. This information will help you continue to hone and refine your skills in this crucial area of meeting leadership.

To gauge your learning, take a few minutes to respond to the following questions:

- In reading this chapter, what did you learn about the importance of emotional connections between staff members?
- What activities did you learn about that will help you to work with your staff members?
- How do awards, games, and other activities work to build emotional connections among staff members?

So far, we have looked at ideas and strategies designed to help you lead energized and effective staff meetings of a short duration (one hour or less). At times, you will be asked to lead longer meetings. These meetings may be scheduled to last anywhere from two hours to a full day. These meetings give you more time with your staff, but they also present unique challenges. In the next chapter, we will present activities that can help you work with staff members for a longer period of time. You will learn strategies that you will find indispensable in making these meetings successful and engaging experiences for your staff members.

6

Extended Meetings . . . When You Have More Time

It takes time to succeed because success is merely the natural reward of taking time to do anything well.

—Joseph Ross

So far, we have outlined techniques and strategies that can be implemented during regular meetings when there is limited time. We all know that short meetings are not the only ones we are asked to conduct; many school leaders are now charged with leading staff development sessions, opening day workshops, retreats, and other meetings that range from half-day to a full day in length. These meetings also need energizing activities to ensure that the people attending them stay focused and have an opportunity to learn. This chapter is devoted to activities designed for meetings that last longer than the typical before- or afterschool staff session.

In this chapter, you will learn about the following:

- The nature of extended meetings and why they need energizing activities
- The staging of energizing activities for a half- or whole-day session
- Activities designed to keep the excitement going all day
- Methods to build collegiality and collaboration in long meetings
- Planning meetings of half- to full-day length
- Ways to evaluate the effectiveness of your half- to full-day session

What Is So Special About Half- or Full-Day Sessions?

Meetings scheduled to last beyond an hour or so bring their own set of challenges. In leading extended meetings, you must take these challenges into account and plan for them. If you don't think through the agenda carefully and plan periodic energizing activities, you and your staff members are in store for a long, boring meeting experience. Here are some of the unique characteristics you need to consider in planning for meetings projected to last longer than one hour:

- Loss of energy: When normally active people are asked to sit for extended periods of time, they can lose energy very quickly. In planning and conducting extended meetings, it is important to take this into consideration and periodically build in natural energizers to maintain focus.

- The need to work together and interact: During extended meetings, people expect that they will be asked to work together. Plan to get your staff members talking and working together as soon as possible after the start of a meeting to get their interactions started. Short, early interaction experiences help people to warm up to working together so that when they need to work together on a longer basis later, they will be ready and able to do so in a collaborative manner.

- The need to pace the meeting processes and content: In any long-term effort, people benefit from pacing themselves to complete the entire experience. Long-distance runners change their speed during the race to ensure a strong finish; the same behavior needs to happen in your extended meetings. It's up to you as the meeting leader to combine fast-paced activities with slow-to-develop ones to provide people with the variety they need to stay focused.

• Breaks: During meetings of long duration, well-timed breaks are essential to effective operation. As the meeting leader, you need to consider the placement of breaks, how much time to allow for them, and how to get people back from their breaks in a positive and timely manner.

• Agenda or meeting script: Most staff members would like to know where the meeting is going, how much time has been allocated to certain parts of the meeting, and when it will be finished. Providing them with a detailed agenda will help them to set their biological clocks and stay focused during the session.

• Organized closing: Because meetings lasting longer than an hour require participants to work together toward larger or more global goals, it is important that they be closed in an organized manner. Many meeting leaders build in a short activity that helps people to summarize the major points of the meeting or generate a list of next steps for continuing what was started in a future meeting.

• Downtime for the meeting leader: When leading a meeting that lasts more than an hour, it is important that you build in activities that will enable you to take a mental break from the group. This not only gives the members a change of pace but also allows to you recharge your batteries and evaluate the progress of the group. Activities may range from simple pair or small-group sharing to more complex group-interaction strategies.

• The need to archive the major points of the meeting: Because you and the participants are spending so much time together, it is important to make some provision for gathering written information from the meeting. Many people learn and remember information better if it is presented both verbally and visually. Make provisions to capture the major points of the meeting visually.

These and other factors can make longer meetings more rewarding and more challenging to implement than short meetings. Keep these factors in mind as you work through the ideas and strategies presented in this chapter.

Building Collegiality and Collaboration

In meetings lasting longer than an hour, it is important to implement activities that build a sense of collaboration and collegiality. In this section, we will share some activities that have worked well for meeting leaders in the past. Some of these activities are designed to be implemented in a short time, whereas others are slower to develop. As you prepare to lead a meeting, consider the length of time that you have to implement activities, the receptivity of your participants, and your own personal comfort before you choose to use them.

With many of these activities, it may seem that you are just "playing games" with your staff. Teachers think that they are wasting their time by playing a game when they feel that they have important work to get accomplished. Be sure that you frame the purpose for spending time on the energizing activity rather than just dropping it on your staff members. Within each activity illustrated in this chapter, you will find an example of how a school leader introduced it to his or her staff members. These real-life illustrations should help you to consider these activities for your staff members.

This Describes Me

At the beginning of a session, group members are asked to introduce themselves to the larger group using an artifact that describes them as a professional. Before the session, teachers are asked to bring an object or artifact that describes them as a teacher, professional, or person. At the beginning of the session, teachers are each given a few minutes to introduce themselves and tell how the artifact they brought describes them. About halfway through the activity, the leader should stop the discussion and ask group members to talk in pairs about what they are learning about each other as a result of the activity. Once this has been done, the activity continues until everyone has had a chance to introduce himself or herself.

Here is an example of how one meeting leader, Ted, used this strategy to build a connection between staff members during an all-day meeting:

Good morning everyone. In the information that I sent you about this meeting, I asked you to bring in an object or an artifact that describes you as a person. We'll take 15–20 minutes at the beginning of the meeting today to give you a chance to introduce yourself to the group using your object or artifact. Take one minute and share your name, your artifact, and how your artifact illustrates something about you.

After all of the participants shared their artifacts, Ted asked members of the group what they had learned about each other as result of the activity. He made note of people's ideas and comments. Several group members commented that even though they had been familiar with some people in the meeting from past interactions, they had learned more personal and important information that they could use as they worked together on the committee task.

This example illustrates how this strategy could be with a group that has some familiarity with each other beyond the scope of the meeting. It can also be used with a group that does not know each other to help them gain knowledge of their colleagues. To use this activity with different groups, vary the prompt that is used to introduce the sharing time. For example, to use this strategy with a group of people who are totally unfamiliar with one another, you might start out with a prompt such as this:

Thanks for coming to this meeting today. I asked you to bring in an artifact that illustrates you as a person or professional. In a minute, I'll ask you to share your artifact. Each person will have two minutes to share the following:

- Your name and your role in the community
- Your artifact and how it illustrates you as a person or professional
- A hope that you have for our meeting today

In this example, the leader asked the participants to tell a little more about themselves and something they hoped would happen during the meeting. The last part of the prompt lets everyone in the group learn more about each person and what he or she expects from the meeting.

The artifact activity builds a positive environment for participants and gets a long meeting off to a positive start. We have found that this activity bonds people together beyond the scope of the meeting. It is fun and motivational for both participants and the leader of the meeting.

Jeopardy!

This version of the popular television game show can set a positive tone for an extended meeting session by allowing your staff members to get to know a little more about each other and the team. This is helpful during an extended staff meeting session because people need to access the strengths of other members to solve problems or to develop new programming ideas. As the leader of a group that is implementing this activity, be sure to share your purpose in implementing this activity with your teachers.

This version of *Jeopardy!* is played using a grid that contains categories, answers, and point values. This grid can be created by using large sheets of poster paper attached to a wall. Along the top of the grid, you list a set of categories, such as travel, career, interest, family, or "who is it?" In the cells below each category, place answers that relate to knowledge about staff members or the organization. An example is provided in Figure 6.1.

Set up the points under each category, like the real game: The first row is worth 100 points, the second row is worth 200 points, the third row is worth 300 points, etc. If you have a hard time thinking of questions or categories, ask your staff members to generate a list.

Divide your staff into equal teams of four or five. Provide each team will a table bell. Have a team pick the first category—for example, "Travel for 100." The leader or moderator reveals the answer in that category. The first team member to ring the bell provides the question to the "answer" that is listed in the category cell. If the team member provides the right question, the team wins the points for that cell. If not, the other teams have an opportunity to ring in and win the points.

The team with the most points at the end of the time period designated for the activity wins the game. This game allows your staff to have fun and learn a little about each other. You can reward the winning team with a small prize.

Here is an example of how Sheila recently introduced this activity to her staff:

It's nice to have everyone together again. In addition to the tasks that we are working on today, I want to use this meeting as an opportunity to strengthen our connections as a team. Today we'll play a game called *Jeopardy!* To play the game, we need to divide up into two teams. The categories are listed on the chart at the front of the room. Get in a single-file line and send your first team member to the front of the room. On the wall chart, seven categories are listed. We'll start with the member from Team A. You can select the category that we will start with. I'll reveal the "answer" to the category. If you think that you know the question that corresponds to the answer, ring your desk bell. If you are first, then you will have the first chance to provide the "answer" to the listed question.

This activity can be both fun and competitive. In some cases, we have used staff information for the general categories; in other cases, we

Figure 6.1   *Jeopardy!* Example Answers and Questions

Answers

Travel	Career	Interest	Family	Who Is It?
August 23	$27,350	Participates in summer concert series out of state as a drummer	Michael, Matt, and Michelle	Was a manager of a clothing store before becoming a teacher
This staff member backpacked across Europe after college	Is a third-generation educator	Glue, balsa wood, paint, and lots of patience	Has a son who works for NASA	Has written columns for a cooking Web site
Disney World	Has held teaching positions in five different schools	*Night at the Roxbury, The Matrix, and Beauty and the Beast*	Bill and Jane	Had a "Home Alone" experience with one of his children on a recent vacation

Questions

Travel	Career	Interest	Family	Who Is It?
What is the date that we need to report for duty next year?	What is the starting salary for a teacher with no previous experience in our district?	What does Bill Sims do during his "off time"?	What are the names of Mel Jordan's three children?	Who is Rhonda White?
Who is Jenny Jones?	Who is Tom Smith?	What does Wanda Bills need to complete a model airplane?	Who is Aaron Levinson?	Who is Steve Smitters?
What place has been visited most by our staff?	Who is Pat Evans?	What films were shown at the three most recent proms?	What are Sue Jones's parents' names?	Who is Paul Major?

have used information pertaining to the meeting we are conducting. Use whatever information you think will provide the most meaning for your staff members as they engage in this activity.

Build a Bridge Together

It is important for staff to work together to solve problems. Sometimes, before tackling a discussion about a complex topic, it is good to start with a mental challenge as a way of warming up to the task. In addition to getting the teachers' minds prepared for a challenge, doing something physical is also fun.

You will need the following materials for this activity:

Two books

Two pieces of 8-1/2 x 11 paper per team

One box of toothpicks per team

A role of masking tape per team

25 pennies per team

A ruler

Give each pair of staff members two books, 50 pennies, and two pieces of paper. The books must be 10 inches apart. Each team must create a bridge out of the piece of paper that spans the distance between the two books. They may fold the paper however they like, but it may not touch the base supporting the books and must rest on top of the books. When they have their bridges built, then they find out how many pennies it can support before the paper either touches the base or the pennies fall off.

As an extension, tell the staff they can use additional materials to strengthen their bridge. Give each team the toothpicks and masking tape; the only rule is that they can't use the tape to attach the ends of the paper to the books.

The team that builds the bridge that holds the most weight is the winner. After the exercise, talk with teams about what they learned about themselves and their team members as a result of the activity. Holding a short discussion helps team members to transfer what they learned to other experiences.

Time Capsule

The time capsule is an activity designed to help a group of teachers to make a successful transition from an existing practice to a new one. By placing items from an existing practice in a time capsule, the are removed from the present view but are not lost entirely. We have found time capsules to be particularly helpful when dealing with transitions:

- Adopting a new reading or language arts series and getting rid of the old series
- Moving into a new building
- Moving into rooms that are different from last year
- Changing the staff-evaluation process
- Adopting a new assessment process
- Dealing with the retirement of staff members
- Helping people to work through a change in leadership
- Changing the instructional strategies used with children
- Helping staff members to implement a new report card
- Helping people move beyond some type of change

In setting up this activity, it is important to let people know that you respect what has happened in the past and that it is important. By using a time capsule, you are helping to preserve an important part of the past while moving into the future. Have teachers talk about the items or artifacts they want to place in the capsule and set a time for the ceremony to occur. Pick up a container that will hold all of the artifacts. Ask each person who is bringing an artifact to be ready to describe the item and its significance to the school. During the ceremony, set a time for the opening of the capsule and bury it on the school grounds.

Putting It Behind Us

This activity is related to the time capsule activity. Because teachers can be especially fond of holding on to old instructional practices or materials after a new curriculum is adopted, this strategy can help them to emotionally detach from their old practices. Ceremonies and processes help people to move beyond their existing comfort zone to new ways of doing business. Here are the steps to make this strategy work:

- Talk with the staff about the importance of moving beyond the old practice and the need to look at new ideas.
- Let the group know that you think it is important for them to have a chance to emotionally process the change in practices from the old to the new.

- One a piece of chart paper, write down the existing or old practice. Divide the paper into two columns; designate one column for the positives of the practice, the other for the negatives of the practice.
- Have the entire group engage in brainstorming ideas for both columns. You can have people meet in small groups first or open up the floor to ideas from the group.
- After all of the brainstormed ideas have been written on the chart, ask the larger group to divide itself into small teams of three or four people to talk about the process and the ideas generated during the exercise.
- On chart paper, list the new innovation or practice to be implemented; list the same two columns that were listed on the first chart.
- Ask the group to brainstorm ideas to fill the chart.
- Have the groups compare the two charts; look for similarities and differences.
- Physically place the old chart in the back of the room and the new chart in the front.
- Ask the group to brainstorm ideas to deal with the negatives identified on the new chart.
- Ask the group to talk about what was learned in the process.

Here's an example of how a meeting leader, Joan, recently debriefed this activity:

Today, we had a chance to look at some of our past practices in working with students. We were able to clearly identify the positive aspects of these practices, but we also identified some areas where these practices have caused us problems. It worked out well to put both the positives and negatives of these practices up on the chart so that we could all examine them more closely. What did you learn from this activity that will help you to implement the new strategies that we examined during the second part of today's meeting?

Toxic Waste Transfer

The toxic waste transfer activity is fun for groups and provides them with valuable information about their operating skills and deficits. It is a favorite activity for both of us, and the groups we have used it with love it as well. It is adapted from an activity described by Midura and Glover in their book *More Team-Building Challenges* (1995).

The group members form a circle around a five-gallon bucket. This bucket has numerous ropes attached to it. The group members must hold on to the ends of the ropes. Working together, the group must transport the bucket from one spot to another by manipulating the ropes. The group also uses these ropes to transfer the contents of the bucket to another container. In transporting or transferring the waste, if any of it spills, the members must elect a waste cleanup specialist who will clean up the waste. The group then must go back to the beginning and start the process over again.

Equipment

To complete this task, you will need to make a toxic waste transfer bucket. Take an empty five-gallon plastic bucket and drill 15–20 small holes randomly and evenly around the sides. Thread ropes of at least 8 feet through the holes, tying a knot at the inside end of each rope. For the toxic waste, fill the bucket with tennis balls, golf balls, Styrofoam peanuts, or other material that can be poured in an efficient manner. Your bucket should look like the example pictured below.

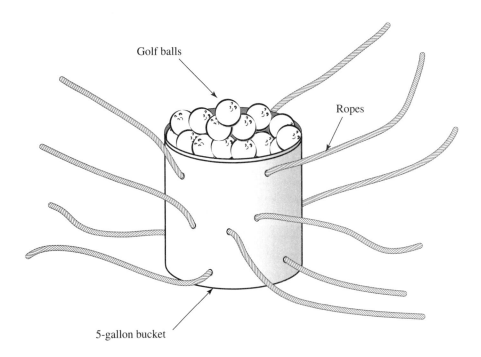

Golf balls

Ropes

5-gallon bucket

Procedure

Place the bucket approximately 50–60 feet from another container that will hold the entire contents of the original bucket. The activity works best when the group has to overcome obstacles (desks, chairs, tables, a hallway, etc.) as they move from the original location to the "dumping site." Discuss the following rules with your group.

- The group can use only the ropes to move and transfer the waste; if a group member touches the bucket or the waste, the group must go back to the beginning and start over.
- Once the group picks up the bucket, it cannot be set down until the waste is completely transferred.
- If any waste spills in the movement or transfer process, the group must select a waste cleanup specialist. This person puts all of the waste back into the original bucket, and the group must start the process all over again from the original starting point.
- Each rope on the bucket must be held by someone, and each person on the team must be touching a rope.
- Team members cannot be closer to the bucket than one-half the length of the rope.

The task is concluded when all of the material has been transferred from the original container to the second container. The facilitator needs to debrief the activity by asking team members to talk about what they learned about each other and the team as a result of this activity.

Keeping Things Revved Up

When you notice your staff members beginning to lose energy during an extended meeting, it is important to insert an energizing activity into the meeting to get them back in sync with the meeting. As you lead, look for indicators such as lethargic behavior, lack of participation, closing eyelids, whispering between participants, and other off-task behaviors. Look for these behaviors after long periods of information dissemination, during the middle of the morning or afternoon, or after a part of the meeting when people have expended a lot of energy.

The following activities can be inserted whenever you notice that the energy level of the group is declining.

Stand and Summarize

When groups of people are required to sit and listen for long periods of time, their thinking can be dulled and they actually can begin to fall asleep. This quick energizer gets people up and moving and engages their bodies in listening and thinking. Here are the steps to remember:

- As the meeting leader, when you notice that group members are having trouble paying attention, stop the meeting.
- Tell everyone to stand up (you can even gesture with your hands).
- Have them find a partner and summarize what they heard in the last 10 minutes and how it affects their professional practice.
- You will notice an immediate surge of energy as people start to talk.
- After two or three minutes, call the group's attention and have everyone sit down again.

Circle Your Thoughts

During some longer sessions, participants may have handouts that help to guide their learning. You can use these as a way to energize a group quickly and effectively. The basic steps for this energizer are the following:

- When you notice that group members are beginning to drift off, ask them to stop.
- Once you have everyone's attention, direct group members to circle or mark in some fashion the two most important points they heard in the last 20 minutes. Give them time to think about their choices.
- Once everyone has marked the most important choices, give them a chance to share their choices with those around them.

Learning Walk

Recently, many authors have commented about the relationship between learning and movement. This strategy allows you to capitalize on movement and energize your group members at the same time. When you notice a group getting sleepy,

- Have the group members stand up.
- Direct them to find a partner whom they can go on a learning walk with during the next two or three minutes.
- Ask the pairs to walk and talk about the most significant aspects they learned in the last 20–30 minutes.

Random Sharing

This activity is closely related to the learning walk but lets participants interact with multiple people in a short period of time. Here are the directions:

- Direct team members to stand up but stay near the spot where they are sitting.
- At the "go" signal, ask them to walk randomly within the room where the meeting is being held. Instruct them that they need to keep walking and moving in a random manner until they hear the signal to stop.
- After the team members have had a chance to move away from familiar peers, say "stop." When the group stops, tell members to find someone who is standing near them to talk with for a minute.
- Give the partners a topic to discuss related to the previous 20–30 minutes of the meeting. Allow them to talk for one to two minutes.
- Instruct the group members to walk around the room in a random manner again until you give them the stop signal again. Repeat the process two or three times, then tell group members to sit down and get ready to learn again.

Follow Me

Sometimes, you just need your group to get up and move around to get them thinking and learning again. This activity is a simple but effective way to reenergize a group and get their thinking engaged again. It does require a little risk taking on the part of group members, so that makes it even more fun. Here are the basic steps involved in this activity:

- Have group members stand and face the front of the room or you, the leader.
- Instruct them that you will be making a series of moves. Their job is to try to follow you as you make each simple move.
- During the first round, have the participants mirror you as you make each movement.
- During the second round, ask participants to stay one movement behind you. For example, if you start off by touching your shoulders, they do nothing. On your second move, if you touch your head, they will touch their shoulders. This process continues and they are challenged to stay one move behind you.

- During the third round, participants are told to remain two moves behind you. If you start off by touching your shoulders, they do nothing. When you move to touch your head, they do nothing. Finally, if your third move is to touch your waist, they touch their shoulders. In this round, people may get confused and start to laugh. It really energizes the group and lets you see them in a vulnerable position.

Squish Ball Review

Throwing and catching can be both challenging and energizing for a group. This activity provides team members a fun way to review and reenergize. The leader provides a squish ball for the group to throw. Members take turns throwing it to each other. When a person catches the ball, he or she must say one thing he or she learned during the meeting. The group members pass the ball around in a random manner until everyone is energized, usually two or three minutes. As the leader, you can have people talk about a variety of topics when the ball is caught. Here are some topics that we have used effectively with groups in the past:

- Share a positive experience from the last two weeks.
- Share a favorite food.
- Give an example of a time when someone on the team helped you.
- Pose a question about the topic of the meeting to the group.
- Brainstorm a suggestion or idea related to the topic of the meeting.
- Share a short, funny incident that happened in the last month.
- Share a new word that you heard during the last six months that was mysterious when you first heard it.
- Share a funny excuse a student has given during the last six months.

Balloon Volleyball

Balloon volleyball helps a group of people to have fun and blow off a little steam. Normally, we don't use it to review or talk about content but to allow people to have fun. It is easy to set up and implement. The leader just needs to provide the balloon and set up a makeshift court in the room.

Divide the group into two teams. Each team must keep the balloon in the air and get it over an obstacle dividing the two groups (such as a desk or an easel) before the balloon touches the floor. The group can hit the balloon as many times as necessary to keep it afloat before hitting it over the "net." Let people play a shortened version of the game to get them up and moving. The fact that the balloon floats around makes it fun and challenging.

Many groups have found it fun to play a variation in which they work together as a team to keep the ball in the air and pass it around without it touching the floor. Group members must hit the ball to keep it in the air and in play. Teachers may be asked to share ideas or examples as they hit the balloon, as they did in the squish ball activity. We have even played a version of this game in which the participants lay on the floor and hit it with their feet. After a few minutes of an energizing activity such as balloon volleyball, the group should be energized and ready to resume their work in the meeting.

Build a Sentence

In this activity, you energize a group by engaging their minds. This activity can be done as a large group, or you can divide the larger group into smaller teams. Here are the steps:

- Ask group members to sit or stand in a semicircle.
- Have everyone face the interior of the semicircle.
- Designate one person to be the starter and assign the rest of the people in the group a participation order.
- Provide the first person with a short phrase to start the activity; the starter adds a word to the original phrase.
- Each person on the team adds a word to build a sentence.
- The last person in the group must finish the sentence so that it makes sense.

The sentences may be related to the content of the meeting, current events, or a random topic generated by the group. If the activity is done using smaller groups, all of the groups should be asked to share their sentences with the larger group at the end of the activity. The activity can be conducted verbally, or the sentence can be written down if it is complex or lengthy.

Dealing With Breaks

Breaks provide your group with needed time away from their task to recharge their batteries and get ready for the next part of the meeting. The biggest problem with breaks is that they often are informally extended well beyond their allotted time limits because participants don't get back to the meeting room on time. Over the course of a day, you might lose 20–30 minutes of valuable meeting time because people don't get back on time. Because this is so common, it is important that you, as the meeting leader, have a provision for helping people get back on time. The following sections describe some ideas that have worked well for others in the past.

Overview of the Break

Take a minute to remind your participants of the purpose of the break and the time allotted for it. Be sure to synchronize the clock in the meeting room with the participants' watches to ensure that everyone has the same time. Here's how a meeting leader recently addressed her group:

In a minute, we will be taking a five-minute break. The purpose of this break is to give you a chance to stand up, use the restroom, and get some refreshments. Because we have a lot to get done today and I know that we want to be ready to leave on time at the end of the day, we need to be back in the room at 10:15. Let's take a second to make sure our watches are in sync with the clock here in the room. We'll see you back again at 10:15.

Partner Reminder

Often, asking participants to be responsible for getting each other back from breaks will improve the timeliness of the group members' return. Before dismissing people on a break, ask them to form pairs. Assign the pairs the responsibility of making sure that both members are back in the room on time. Your directions to the group may sound like this example from a meeting leader who recently led an extended-day meeting:

You have been working very hard today. We need to take short break to reenergize ourselves, but I need you to be back on time. Take a minute and form yourselves into pair teams. As a pair, talk about how you will make sure that both of you are back in the room and ready to move on with our meeting in 10 minutes. Because we will use the clock in this room as our official timekeeper, be sure to synchronize your watches with this clock. I'll see you back here at 10:25.

Leaders to Get Everyone Back on Time

Meeting leaders can help participants to feel a sense of responsibility for their peers by assigning several of them to be responsible for getting others back from the break in a timely manner. This strategy has worked well in the past and can take the pressure off the leader to round everyone up when the break is over. It can be fun and novel to provide some energy for the group members as they work to get everyone back on time. Here's an example of how a meeting leader used this idea recently:

We are going to take a 10-minute break. It is important that we get back here on time because we have a lot to take care of before the end of the day. To help get everyone back, I have asked the following people to help act as timekeepers. They will let you know when there is about one minute left in the break and that it is time to return to the meeting room. Let's make sure that we all have the same time according to the meeting room clock. We'll see you back here at 10:30.

Incentives to Return

Some meeting leaders find it energizing to give incentives or prizes to people who return on time after a break. In using this strategy, be sure to think of an incentive that is simple but allows everyone to win if they are back on time. For example, you could consider one of the following ideas:

- Closing the meeting a few minutes early if a certain percentage of the group is back on time.
- Offering some small token when people are back on time, such as a pencil, marker, or other prize.
- Placing everyone's name who is back on time in a box and holding a drawing for a medium-sized prize at the end of the day.

Here's how one meeting leader recently used this strategy during a meeting he was leading:

To make the kind of progress that we need to make today, it is important that we get back on time from our break in 10 minutes. For those of you back at 2:30, I have a small prize that I'll give to you. Go ahead and take a break and we'll see you back here in 10 minutes.

Music to Call People Back

Another energizing way to get people to come back to a meeting on time is to use music. At the beginning of a break, you can announce that when there are approximately three minutes left in the break, you will play a certain song. When the song is over, everyone needs to be in their seats and ready to get started again with the meeting. This strategy has worked exceptionally well in the past with a variety of meetings. It is important that, as the meeting leader, you make sure that you start and end the song on time. Be sure to think about how you will make sure that this happens on cue. Here's an example of how this worked in actual practice:

We have a 10-minute break coming up soon. It is important that we are back here on time and ready to begin our meeting. To help you get back, when there are about three minutes left, I will be playing the *Rocky* theme song. When it is finished, you need to be in your seat and ready to begin. Have a great break and we'll see you back here at 2:45.

Assigned a Task to Be Completed at the Start of the Next Session

Group members tend to be on task for the most part. Use this tendency to help you energize your participants and get them back from breaks on time. If you give them a task to complete right after the break, it will get people back on time and reengaged. In using this technique, we usually write the assigned task on chart paper before people are dismissed for the break. The strategy works best when people have a task to complete as a group. This helps to reinforce the collaborative tone that you are trying to set in your meeting. Here is an example of how we recently used this strategy:

As we get ready for our break, I want to share what we will do when we return. On the chart is an assignment that I want you to complete with your small group teams. You need to return from the break at 10:40 and work as a group for 10 minutes to complete the assigned task. At 10:50, all of the groups will share the product of their work with the whole staff. We will use what your team generates during the next part of our session.

A variation of this technique that we have used successfully with groups is to allow time for the break and the work assignment all together. We give the small teams the assignment and share the time schedule, then allow each team to complete the assignment and take a break any time within the larger time frame. We have found that some small-group team members like to finish their task before taking a break, some like to complete a part of it before breaking, and others will take a break and then complete the assignment. The flexibility of this idea usually eliminates the long lines at the break table and restrooms that can make people late in returning from their breaks.

Here's how the strategy was implemented with a group we recently led:

In a minute, we will be taking a short break. We also need to complete the following task in small groups. As a small group, you can decide how you want to spend your time. You need to take a break and complete the task within a 20-minute time period. If you want to take your break and then return to work on the task, that is OK. If you want to work on the task and then take a break, that is OK also. Your small group needs to be sure to complete the task, take a break, and be ready to share the result of your work by 10:50. Have a great break!

Staging Energizing Activities for Maximum Impact

For sessions of an hour or more, you should introduce your participants to simple, easy activities, then gradually ask them to complete more complex energizing tasks. Starting off with simple activities helps your staff become accustomed to the idea of participating before you ask them to complete more difficult energizers. You also may find that people in your group need to warm up to the idea of doing energizers.

You may have them talk in pairs or triplets as an opening activity. As you watch them participate, you can begin to introduce activities that require more involvement and risk taking on their part. If you stage your energizers properly, you will find that people are willing to be involved in activities that require a lot of them by the middle of the meeting. If you move into complex energizers too soon, you may meet some resistance.

Planning Strategies

When planning long meetings, there are several things to keep in mind. Figure 6.2 provides a template that you may want to use in

Figure 6.2   Planning Template for Long Meetings

Meeting Phases and Needs	Possible Strategies	Ways to Measure Effectiveness
Opening the meeting		
Providing opportunities for group members to work together		
Providing downtime for the meeting leader		
Pacing the meeting processes and content		
Providing timely breaks		
Avoiding the loss of energy by group members		
Providing an organized closing		
Evaluating the effectiveness of the meeting		

planning your next long meeting. As you fill in the grid, be sure to use the strategies and ideas that you have learned so far in this book.

Summary

Conducting a half- or full-day meeting doesn't have to be a difficult task if you think about using energizing activities to help your teachers learn and to break up the content of the day. In this chapter, we examined some energizing activities that lend themselves to meetings longer than one hour. In addition to these activities, we also had a chance to look at strategies that enable a group to be productive and waste less time by getting people back promptly from breaks. As many meeting leaders know, it is easy for a group to inadvertently stretch a 10-minute break into 20–25 minutes of downtime. The strategies presented in this chapter should help to minimize this problem. Finally, we introduced a template to assist meeting leaders as they plan meetings lasting longer than one hour. Some of the major considerations that need to be taken into account when planning a lengthy meeting are included in this template.

As you complete this chapter, take a few minutes to respond the following questions:

- How do long meetings differ from short meetings of an hour or less?
- Why is it important to have a clear strategy in mind for getting people back from breaks?
- What strategies and activities did you learn that hold promise for improving your meetings?
- How do you plan to change the next extended meeting that you are planning?

In the next chapter, "Closing the Meeting With a Bang," we will look at ideas to help you end your meetings. Just like the beginning, the ending of a meeting is also a crucial time for leaders because many people remember the closing and draw their opinions about the meeting from how it ends. Another important aspect of the closing of a meeting is that this is the time when a group normally decides its progress and sets up a calendar for future meetings together. As the leader of a group, you want people to take what they gained and learned during the meeting into other situations. In the next chapter, you will find strategies that you can implement quickly and easily to make your next meeting meaningful and end with a bang.

7

Closing the Meeting With a Bang

When you come to the end of your rope, tie a knot and hang on.

—Franklin Delano Roosevelt

E nergized meetings have powerful endings. People normally remember two parts of a meeting: the beginning and the end. If you want to build a culture of energized staff meetings, you will need to provide opportunities for people to end them on a high note. In this chapter, we will focus on strategies and activities that will help you close your meetings with a sense of purpose and meaning.

In this chapter, you will learn the following strategies to help you close your meetings with a bang:

- Simple and easy-to-implement activities that will put the icing on the cake of your meetings
- Methods to help a group tie into positive emotions to close down a meeting and transfer their experiences to another meeting

- Ways to sum up the information learned at a meeting so that it can be used again in the future
- Ideas to carry the enthusiasm from this meeting to the end of the session; ways to keep everyone engaged until the end
- Strategies to use this previously untapped source of time in a productive and meaningful manner

Why End With a Bang?

Imagine how you would feel if you were at an orchestra concert, listening to an energetic and inspiring piece of music, when all of a sudden, the energy of the song tailed off and it ended in a bland fashion. Think about your reaction if you were watching a suspenseful and engaging movie and, right before the climax, it ended with a dull and predictable closing.

In both of these examples, the listener or viewer experienced what many people who attend meetings have to deal with all of the time—a lackluster or dull ending. Because participants do remember endings, when they experience a boring ending, they will remember that as they reflect on the meeting. Let's take a look at some of the more common implications when a leader lets a meeting just end with little or no emotion.

People Perceive That the Leader Lacks Skills

When teachers attend meetings, they attribute the effectiveness of the meeting to the skills of the leader. This is especially true in cases of poorly conducted meetings. Some teachers may even say, "If that is the best that she can run a meeting, how can she expect me to do a good job teaching my students?" We have known many fine school leaders who developed a negative reputation because of the way they led their meetings.

Meeting Participants Anticipate the End and Shut Down Their Thinking

When meetings just tail off and close in mundane ways, people begin to anticipate the end and start to prepare to leave. This preparatory behavior may have a negative impact on a group because some important decisions occur at the end of a meeting. In some cases, people have shut down so much that they actually start to leave the meeting before it is finished. In extreme cases, the shutdown time keeps moving back, week after week, until participants come to the meetings already in shutdown mode.

Good Ideas or Momentum Can Be Lost

When meetings end on a low energy level, it can become very hard for participants to remember what resolutions were worked out during the productive part of the meeting. People usually benefit from some kind of emotional trigger that helps them to lock significant information into their long-term memories. When there is a lack of emotion, it is harder for the brain to store and retrieve significant information.

Specific Strategies to End Meetings With a Bang

In this section, you will learn ideas and strategies that can be used to end your meetings with some emotional connection. All of these strategies will work with different groups at different times. You may be comfortable with some and uncomfortable with others. You need to use your judgment when selecting ideas to use with your own staff. Next to each idea, the typical amount of time that is spent on the strategy is listed. This will help you as you plan your agenda because you will know how much time to set aside for the activity.

Replay It in Your Mind (2–3 minutes)

With this strategy, the leader asks participants to revisit key points that were made during the meeting and reflect on how these points affected their thinking. It is a simple exercise but causes people's minds to review the material from the meeting. Not only is this strategy a good way to help people to remember the major points of a meeting, but it is also low key enough for most people to feel comfortable participating. After you give your group members about 30 seconds to think about the key points of the meeting, it is a good idea to ask them to share their thoughts with another person. This allows participants to further reinforce the key points of the meeting and raises the level of accountability because they have to share their thoughts with someone else.

It is important to properly phrase your question and then stop to let people reflect on the key points of the meeting. Here are some prompts you may consider using:

- Take a minute and think about two key points that are important to remember about our meeting today.
- Before we leave for the day, replay the three most important pieces of information you learned from today's meeting.
- In your head, review the agenda from the meeting; identify two or three of the most critical aspects.
- Pretend that you have been asked to share the two most important things you learned from our meeting today. Identify those and be ready to share them with someone else in the room.
- Imagine you have been asked to summarize the meeting today. What two or three points would you tell someone who was not here?
- As you reflect on today's meeting, what important ideas do you want to remember for future use?
- In your head, repeat the most important idea from today's meeting, the next most important, and the third most important. What do all of these ideas have in common?
- Picture in your mind the two most critical topics from today's meeting.

All of these prompts could be used to encourage people to reflect on the most critical aspects of the meeting. Be sure to say the prompt and then give people 20 to 40 seconds to think and reflect. After this reflection time, it is a good idea to ask them to form groups of two or three and have them share their major points.

Zig Zag Passing (2–3 minutes depending on the size of the group)

This activity can be a fun way to close a meeting. It involves the sharing of ideas coupled with the passing of a beach ball. Here's how it works:

- Ask the participants to form pairs.
- Have members of the pair groups line up across from each other, forming two single parallel lines (see Figure 7.1).
- Label one of the lines A and the other B.
- Start at one end of Line A; ask the first person in line to share one thing that was significant about the meeting with the entire group. After this person shares, have him or her pass the beach ball to a person in Line B, who catches the ball and then shares a significant happening from the meeting.

Figure 7.1   Zig Zag Passing

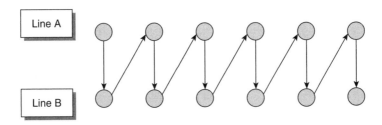

- Alternate the sharing and passing of the beach ball between Lines A and B, moving down the line until all of the members have shared a significant idea. The diagram in Figure 7.1 illustrates the passing pattern that is used for this activity.
- After everyone has shared, talk as a group about what was learned from the activity.

Rotating Circles (3–4 minutes)

This simple activity helps people to share the major points from a meeting in an enjoyable manner. It has the advantage of helping people to review the major points from the meeting while maintaining accountability by asking them to share their ideas with others. This activity is also fairly low key in the level of participation that it requires. It basically works like this:

- Ask the people at your meeting to form groups of two.
- Each small group needs to designate one member as Person A and the other as Person B.
- All of the A members sit in a circle facing outward.
- All of the B members sit in a circle surrounding the inner circle facing their partners (see Figure 7.2).
- Ask Person A to share one or two highlights from the meeting with Person B.
- Ask Person B to share one or two highlights from the meeting with Person A.
- After one minute, ask the people in the B group to move one chair clockwise.
- With the new partners, repeat the A and B sharing.
- If there is time, rotate the B group again and repeat the process.
- Ask all group members what they learned from the process.

Figure 7.2 Rotating Circles

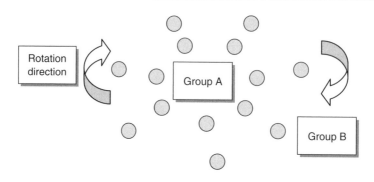

The Information Frenzy

This activity is another low-key way of asking your participants to review the major content of the meeting both in their minds and verbally. It was introduced in John's book, *Effective Group Facilitation in Education* (Eller, 2004). It can be a fun and challenging way to provide for a quick review. Here are the major steps in the process:

- Ask team members to divide themselves into pairs.
- In the pair groups designate a Person A and a Person B.
- Person A talks for 45 seconds and shares everything that he or she can remember about the meeting. During this time, Person B can only listen.
- After the 45 seconds have expired, the leader stops the activity.
- Person B now shares everything that he or she remembers from the meeting. Person B cannot repeat anything that Person A said.
- After 45 seconds, the leader stops the activity.
- The game moves to a second round in which both pair members are asked to repeat the format of the first round. No pair member can repeat anything that was said by another pair member or shared in a previous round. The time limit for the second round is 30 seconds for each person to share.
- At the end of the second round, the leader stops the activity.
- The game moves to a third round. The same process is followed, but this round lasts for 15 seconds per person.
- At the end of the three rounds, the leader lets both pair members talk about any unfinished topics and their impressions of the activity.

The information frenzy is a popular activity that we use in our work with schools and school systems. You will find that the conversations become richer as people go through the exercise. The ideas shared by one partner tend to stimulate thoughts in the other partner.

Visual Representations

Another way for a group to review the major points of a meeting is to have members develop visual representations that sum up the major learning or the major ideas expressed in the meeting. This activity can be done by individuals or small groups, but it is highly effective in helping group members to see the results of the meeting. Here is how it can work in a group:

- Divide the larger group into smaller teams of three to six members.
- Provide chart paper and markers to each small team.
- Assign the teams to develop a visual representation that sums up what was insightful for them or represents the major points of the meeting. Give the groups 5–10 minutes to complete their representation.
- At the end of the construction phase, ask each team to share its visual representation with the larger group. Make sure the teams explain their representations and provide clarification for the larger group.
- Ask team members to talk about what they learned as a result of the activity and how they could use it in their classrooms to help their students sum up their learning.

Gallery Display

This closing activity provides participants an opportunity to see what progress was made during the session and also gives them a light emotional experience. It is built on the concept of an art gallery in which artists display their works. People walk through an art gallery to see and experience the best of an artist's work; the meeting gallery display is designed to provide the people who attended the meeting a chance to see the best of their work. It can use visuals and graphics that the group creates (such as visual representations) or charts that were generated as a part of the meeting. Here are the basic steps to create the gallery display:

- Post the work that was accomplished during the meeting around the room (either the charts generated during the meeting or visuals that small teams constructed).
- Divide the larger group into pairs.
- Ask the pairs to walk around the gallery and talk about what they see and learn from walking through the display.
- After everyone has had a chance to walk through the display, hold a large-group discussion about the evidence people looked at and the progress made by the large group on the tasks or goals of the meeting.

Gallery displays also can be used to showcase the work of small teams or task forces, to help people see all of the parts of a problem or solution, or to help a group sum up the progress made during a short segment of the day (such as a part of a morning session). We have found that when they are used properly, gallery displays help a group to truly understand its progress and to build an emotional connection to each other and the meeting process.

Charting Our Progress

This is a simple and energizing activity that groups have found motivating and enlightening. It takes little up-front preparation but helps a group to really see how much ground it covered during the meeting. It unfolds like this:

- At the end of the meeting, the leader posts pieces of chart paper around the room that contain prompts for group members to write their reactions as a team (see Figure 7.3 for example prompts).
- The meeting leader subdivides the larger group into smaller teams of two or three people.
- Each team is assigned to stand by one of the charts.
- At the "start" signal, the teams write a response to the prompt, which relates to the content of the meeting or extends the content of the meeting. Sample prompts include the following:

  What were the two most import points made during the meeting today?

  What was accomplished that surprised you in the meeting today?

  Write an adjective that describes your feelings about the meeting today.

What do you wish we had addressed more fully at the meeting today?

How do you think we accomplished so much in our meeting today?

What action steps does the group need to take now that we have moved this far toward a solution?

- After two to three minutes, the meeting leader stops the teams and asks them to move to the next chart in a clockwise manner, and begin writing about the new prompt (see the section on carouseling in Chapter 4 for more details about movement procedures).
- The teams continue to move around the room until they have answered all of the prompts or the meeting leader senses that the group has lost energy.
- Once all of the charts are completed, give participants a chance to walk around the room and review them. Ask them to talk about what they learned as a result of the activity.

Figure 7.3 Chart Prompt Examples

✓ What do you feel were the three greatest accomplishments of our meeting today?

✓ What item or idea "fit" the best with you from our meeting today?

✓ How do you see our work together as a starting point for more progress in the future?

✓ What happened today that made you the most optimistic?

✓ What happened today that made you the most pessimistic?

✓ Describe our time together in this meeting using only one word.

✓ Our meeting today was like . . .

✓ Our meeting today reminded me of the movie _____ because _____.

✓ We're glad we did _____ today because _____.

✓ We wish we would have done _____ today because_____.

✓ We saw _____ in a new light as a result of _____ today.

✓ We are more _____ as a result of our meeting.

✓ A metaphor for our work together today could be _____.

✓ A problem is to a solution as our work today is to _____ (this is an analogy).

Spin and Win

This activity provides some fun and excitement for staff members and helps to close down a meeting with a bang. In involves a roulette-type spinning wheel with prizes listed on it. Sheila has used wheels that were either made by her parent organization or bought for school carnivals as the main spinning wheel for the activity.

At the end of the meeting, announce that you will be spinning for a number of prizes. Sheila normally draws out three or four teacher names to spin the wheel, and they win the prize that the wheel stops at. Here are examples of some of the prizes that typically are given away in this type of activity:

Ticket or coupon to get out of duty free

Book

$25 certificate to buy supplies for the classroom

School t-shirt

School hat

Lottery ticket

Candy

Certificate that allows them to have their classroom covered for one hour

Desk supplies

Some of the prizes are provided by the school's parent organization, and others come out of the school store or the school budget. Sheila, for example, covers the duties of those who win prizes. Covering classes or job assignments builds goodwill with staff members and lets them know that you care about them. It also gives you a chance to see how things really work in the school.

Frame the Day

In this energizing activity, meeting participants are asked to construct a frame around the major accomplishments or learning of the meeting. Because it involves the team members in building something and presenting a project, it brings natural energy to the group. Here is how it unfolds with a group:

- Divide the larger group into smaller teams or three or four people.
- Provide each team with several sheets of paper, construction paper, and markers.
- Give each team several minutes to construct a drawing or picture that sums up the major accomplishments or learning from the meeting. Teams can use some of the construction paper provided to construct a frame for their picture, or the pictures can be presented without a frame.
- At the end of the work time, ask team members to do a short (30-second) presentation of their "works of art."
- At the end of the presentations, ask the larger group to vote on the top three artworks. The winners can be mounted in small frames purchased from a discount store.
- Award small prizes to the winners.
- Talk about what was learned as a result of this activity.

If you like, you also could have the group do a gallery display of all of their frames. Use the same process that was outlined in the gallery display activity described earlier in this chapter.

Video Clips

A favorite activity that we use to close a meeting is a short video clip that relates to the meeting or illustrates something that we want participants to take away from the experience. These short clips usually last two to three minutes but pack in a lot of powerful images and a clear message to the meeting participants. Because all commercial video clips are copyrighted, we usually rent the entire video and cue it to the appropriate spot on the tape for the meeting.

Here is a sample of some of the clips that we have used recently and the messages that we wanted our participants to take away from the meeting.

When and How to Use Video Clips

Movie	Segment	Message to Take Away
Forrest Gump	Scene in which Forrest is called back from his shrimp boat because his mother is dying, to the point when he gives a share of his money to Bubba's mother	Destiny: What is your destiny as a teacher? What do you want your destiny to be?
Dances With Wolves	Scene in which John Dunbar first meets Stands With Fist and Kicking Bird and the three parties try to communicate with each other	Listening and understanding: What did the people in the clip do to understand each other? What do we need to do to understand and learn from each other?
The Out-of-Towners (with Goldie Hawn and Steve Martin)	Scene in which the couple is in the police station after having been arrested in Central Park; Goldie Hawn tries to use the station phone; she gets angry with the watch officer after he says "Give me a break"	Customer service: How can we understand the perspectives that others (parents) bring to the table? How can we listen and work with them?
Apollo 13	Scene in which the engineers are asked to fix the carbon dioxide scrubbers; they dump all of the parts on the table and are asked to devise a solution to the problem	"Can do" attitude: What do we need to do to solve this problem as a staff? What resources do we have in place to address the situation?
My Best Friend's Wedding	Scene in which George meets the bride's parents at the church, joins the family for lunch, and sings "I'll Say a Little Prayer for You"	How can we change our conversation style to meet the needs of our listeners?

Summary

Great meetings have energizing beginnings and endings—we started this chapter with that general idea. The end of a meeting tends to stick in people's minds; therefore, it is crucial to the success of a meeting that the ending activities build a positive feeling among participants. In this chapter, you were exposed to a wide variety of activities that can energize staff at the end of a meeting and help people to draw conclusions and sum up their learning from the meeting. As you move forward in trying some of these ideas, keep in mind that you may feel a little uncomfortable implementing them at first, but in the long run, they are good for staff members. Many times, time constraints will tempt you to leave out a closing, but doing so will shortchange the process and make your meeting a less-than-powerful experience. We hope that after reading this chapter, you understand the importance of meeting closings and feel confident in implementing several good ideas.

Think about your answers to the following questions to check your learning about the concepts and ideas presented in this chapter:

- What two or three ideas or strategies did you pick up in this chapter that will help you to improve the closings of your meetings?
- What considerations need to be taken into account when closing a meeting?
- How can you get your staff more involved in interacting with the main ideas from the meeting as a closing activity?

In Chapter 8, "Closing Thoughts and Next Steps," you will step back and look at the big picture of improving and energizing your meetings. In addition to examining five crucial steps in faculty development, you also will learn how to spot and deal with the staff resistance that can occur when leaders make changes to improve their meetings. The ideas presented in this chapter have been valuable for us and for the school leaders whom we have helped to improve their schools over the years. This chapter will tie together all that you have learned and help you implement energizing activities to make your meetings a success!

8

Closing Thoughts and Next Steps

The toughest thing about success is that you've got to keep on being a success.

—Irving Berlin

N ow that you have read this book and learned about energizing your staff meetings, it's important to think about the most important phases of the process: implementation and follow-up. This idea my sound logical and straightforward, but many good ideas are left on the drawing board because people don't think through the foundation and strategies needed to move them forward. In this chapter, we will look at important considerations that you need to think about if you are serious about changing your staff meetings.

Step 1: Understand Your Strengths, Weaknesses, and Inhibitions

This concept was discussed at the very beginning of the book, but it is crucial to know your capabilities before you start to move forward.

Even though most of the ideas and strategies we have discussed in this book are grounded in common sense, you should know enough about the concept of energizing meetings to feel confident in moving forward. If you are feeling a little shaky, reread some of the chapters to reground yourself in the content and to boost your confidence in trying new ideas. Talk with other leaders about your understanding of energizing meetings; involve lead teachers in helping you move forward to improve your meetings. Take a little extra time to make sure that you feel confident and competent; the time spent will benefit you in the long run.

Step 2: Build a Seedbed

Farmers take time to make sure the ground has just the right amount of nutrients and moisture to ensure the crops they plant have a chance to grow successfully. You should do the same with your staff and school before starting your project. Your school's seedbed can be nurtured in a variety of ways. Here are some of the most common methods we have used in our work with schools over the years:

- Talk with key staff members about the need to improve meetings.
- Form a committee to study the effectiveness of meetings.
- Talk with the entire faculty about the need to improve meetings.
- Provide teachers with articles about energized staff meetings and how they can help a group.
- Form a principal's advisory team and ask the team to study the importance and implementation of energized staff meetings.
- Provide copies of this book to key staff members so that they can read about and understand the importance of energized staff meetings.
- Start to implement short icebreakers at the beginning of staff meetings, and then explain how to duplicate these icebreakers in classrooms. After teachers try them, check their perceptions of how they affected the teachers, both as participants and as teachers with their students.

Step 3: Plant the Seeds

Once the seedbed is prepared, the farmer actually starts the growth process by planting the seeds. In your effort to energize your staff meetings, this is called the *initial implementation phase*. Starting out right will be crucial to the success of your project. Get prepared and ready to go. The implementation phase of energizing your staff meetings may look different in schools depending on the needs of your staff members. Here are some examples of how some schools have launched their energizing efforts:

- A principal talked briefly about the benefits of energized staff meetings and then involved the staff members in a short, simple-to-implement activity and asked for staff reaction.
- In an elementary school, the principal worked with two teachers to help them learn about energized staff meetings. He had them introduce the concept to the teachers and start on a short introductory activity.
- At a high school, the principal worked with the department chairs to teach them energizing activities and strategies. She asked them to try out the ideas they had learned during their department meetings. Once she was sure that every faculty member had experienced energizing activities in his or her department, she implemented activities in the large-group faculty meetings.
- An elementary principal learned about energizing strategies over the summer and decided to use them during the opening-day workshop. He completely changed the room arrangement and the format for the opening day, integrating energizers throughout the day.
- A principal recently launched an energizing change by bringing in an outside consultant to start the process during a beginning-of-the-year workshop. He asked for staff perceptions about the experience after the session.

Step 4: Nurture Them, Watch Them Grow

For a seed to become a full-grown plant, it needs to be nurtured. As the leader, there are lots of ways to nurture your staff members as they learn to work together in an energized meeting setting. Here are a few that we have seen or used in our work with schools:

- The principal thanks the staff for their participation in energized activities.
- The leader points out the growth that he or she has seen in the staff as a result of the energizing activities.

- Staff members are taught to reinforce each other for the meetings-improvement efforts.
- The group leader provides extra release time as a reward for the work that the planning team has done to implement energizing activities.
- Pictures of staff members engaging in energizing activities are taken.
- The principal mentions the implementation of energizing activities and their use in meetings in the school newsletter.
- The leader comes to classrooms to demonstrate how some of the activities used in meetings can be used with students to help them in their learning.
- The principal invites district personnel to come to staff meetings to see how the energizing meetings work.
- Rewards or prizes are given to teachers for their participation.

Step 5: Pull the Weeds

After a time, problems with your implementation may arise. These problems can be like weeds in a garden or farm field. Left unchecked, weeds can choke the best of gardens; likewise, problems can choke your best efforts to implement energized staff meetings.

Problems can take many forms; the most common problems that we see in our work with schools that are implementing energized staff meetings include the following:

- Negative staff members who undermine your efforts (implementation blockers)
- Teachers who want to see change but are reluctant to "stick their necks out"
- Staleness (using the same strategies over and over)
- Lack of time to fully implement energizing activities
- Principal or leader who drops the ball and never follows through on promises or expectations
- Lack of connection between energizing activities, the improved processes of meetings, and teachers' strategies to address problems (weeds). Nobody understands why they are implementing energizing activities. Eventually, people begin to think the activities are a waste of time and not worth their effort.

Like weeds in a garden, problems start out small but quickly turn into major issues. It's best to address them when you first notice their appearance. By "pulling" them early, you can avoid larger issues down the road.

Negative Staff Members Who Undermine Your Efforts (Implementation Blockers)

These kinds of people can be particularly damaging to your efforts in energizing your staff meetings. Their comments and actions tend to draw in others who still may be skeptical about your efforts. If they are direct with you, they can meet with you and you can address their concerns. By directly questioning your ideas, they may provide you with valuable questions that need to be asked about your energizing efforts. See how Peggy handles a confrontational teacher in the following example:

One of Peggy's teachers, Mike, expressed that he felt the energizing activities in meetings were a waste of time and stupid. Peggy was able to set up a follow-up meeting with Mike to clarify the situation. During the meeting, Peggy listened to Mike and found out that he had some valid points. As a result of her meeting with him, she took the time to explain the purpose behind the various activities in the staff meetings. She reminded teachers of the purpose before each new activity. This helped Mike to see the relevance and provided information related to the process of energizing activities for all of the staff.

In this example, the teacher was open about his resistance to the use of energizing activities. Peggy was able to deal with the problem directly and get Mike on board. What about people who work behind the scenes to undermine your efforts to improve your staff meetings? Dealing with covert blockers could be the topic of a whole book, but, in general, there are some ways to attack the problem. Let's look at a few ideas.

The Nature of Implementation Blockers

"Implementation blockers" is a term that we use to describe people on the staff who like the fact that things never change. These people may benefit in some manner from the status quo. They will work behind the scenes to undermine some very well-intended efforts by you and other staff members to move the group forward. There are some key behaviors that can tip you off that you have an implementation blocker on your hands:

- Eye rolling during meetings when energizing activities are introduced
- Looking at one or two other people consistently in a skeptical manner during energizing activities
- Appearing to laugh or snicker when you, the leader, introduce energizing activities
- Meeting in small groups before a meeting; these small groups stop talking when you come near them
- Hesitating to move when directed to change groups or activities during the meeting
- One or two members acting as the "spokesperson" for the entire group; this spokesperson makes comments or brings forth assertions that undermine the meeting improvement strategies. Some of these comments could include the following:

> "Many of us on the faculty feel that these activities are a waste of time."

> "I spoke to the parent group and they agree with our concerns."

> "All of the staff members I have spoken to have some concerns about this new effort."

Implementation blockers will try to get you to abandon your meeting-improvement efforts by undermining your confidence in your leadership and the meeting strategies you are implementing. Here is a way to deal with their comments:

- Listen to the message, ask clarifying questions, and seek to understand the origin of the concern. Normally, implementation blockers cannot back up their assertions when pressed for specificity.
- Listen to the core of their comments to see whether they have any merit. Address those ideas right away.
- Listen to the language that implementation blockers use; analyze it for specificity. Normally, they will be very vague or general in their description of their concern.
- Be ready to share the big picture and the supporting details of your efforts. Even if you don't think that they will agree with you or believe you, share your overall plan. If you are specific, it can take some of the bite out of their arguments.
- Agree to check in with them at a future date to see whether they still have concerns.

Covert Resistance

Normally, you will find out about people who are talking behind your back through some method. From our experiences, many times, other teachers who support you will confide in you. In these cases, you must move forward carefully. It is important to confront the situation without giving away how you found out the person was talking behind your back. See how Howard handles this situation in the following example:

Thanks for meeting with me today, Joan. I am talking with staff members to see what their reactions are to the new meeting structures we have put in place. What are your thoughts, especially your concerns regarding the new activities? [Joan shares two or three concerns.] Thanks for sharing your thoughts. I am glad that you came to me rather than go around talking about your concerns. When we meet we can usually work things out.

Even though this conference was simple, Joan got the message that Howard knew she was upset about the new meeting ideas. Howard's approach let Joan know that he knew she was up to something. If Joan had said that she had no concerns about the meeting changes, Howard could have said, "If you ever have any concerns, I'll expect you to meet with me first so that we can work things out before bigger troubles arise." We have found this approach works with people who work behind the scenes to undermine your efforts. At times, we have had to directly confront these underminers, but usually we save that strategy for a last resort. When you confront people, they are able to go to their support group and share that you are picking on them. Howard's subtle approach let Joan know that he knew and helped to remind her of the proper procedures for dealing with concerns.

Teachers Who Want to See Change but Are Reluctant to "Stick Their Necks Out"

This problem can be fairly common in faculties that are implementing new ideas. Moving toward energized faculty meetings can be a risk-taking experience for people. Here are some strategies to help people gain the courage they need to move forward:

- Provide a safety net for your staff by letting them know what you are planning to do in their meetings and how they can "opt out" if they fear bodily harm or personal embarrassment.
- Encourage teachers by reassuring them that the activities will cause them no harm or embarrassment.
- Reinforce people for their efforts, no matter how small.
- Participate in the activities as much as possible.
- If you know that you have sensitive staff members, resist laughing or making funny comments that could be misunderstood during their initial trials with the new activities.
- Talk with more comfortable teachers about how they can support teachers who are reluctant to participate.
- Meet with people you know are reluctant before the meeting to explain the upcoming activities. Let them have a chance to share their concerns.

Staleness (Using the Same Strategies Over and Over)

Be sure to vary the ideas and activities that you use in energizing your staff meetings. A variety of activities have been presented in this book to give you a good start in energizing your group.

Lack of Time to Fully Implement Energizing Activities

Be sure to provide ample time in your agenda to allow the activities to be fully implemented. It is important to make sure that you provide your group with time to debrief the activities as well.

Step 6: Harvest the Crop

If you work carefully with your staff, you will reap the benefits of your energizing efforts. You will find that your staff members are better able to work together in a collaborative manner, solve problems, and work to improve the school. In harvesting the crop, you will find that your teachers will develop a need to assume more leadership roles in the school. This increased leadership capacity doesn't mean that you will be out of a job—it means that your teachers can take ownership of the success.

Once you notice there is a need for an increased level of ownership, you can satisfy this need and continue to build your teachers' capacities by engaging them in the following activities:

- Allow teachers to conduct some of the energizing activities that are implemented during your staff meetings.
- Have a team of staff members get together and plan staff meetings.
- Form small special teams and task forces; allow team leaders to plan and conduct these meetings. You can attend as a participant.
- Ask interested staff members to conduct parent group meetings; they can facilitate sections of the meetings.
- Have teachers conduct the feedback portions of your meetings.
- Let teachers gather data about the energizing efforts outside staff meetings; have them summarize the results and present them at the next meeting.
- Ask teams of teachers who appear to be interested in increased leadership opportunities how they would like to move forward.

Summary and Send-Off

In this book, we touched on the topic of energizing your staff meetings and other ideas related to this effort. We presented ideas and activities that you can use in a variety of situations. We also gave you some strategies to deal with special cases and situations that you may face as you work to make your staff meetings more engaging for your staff members.

As a way of checking your understanding of the strategies presented in this chapter, take a minute to think about your answers to the following questions:

- Why is convert resistance damaging to groups, and how can you bring it out into the open?
- How can you "build the seedbed" to help your staff as you move forward in improving your meetings?
- What did you learn from this chapter and from this book that will benefit you as you work to improve your meetings?

Keep in mind that you are the best judge of how to move forward on this effort with your staff. Although the ideas and activities presented in this book have worked for thousands of people over the years, you need to think about each one before you put it into place to see how it will work for you and your staff. Reflection and context building will be important as you move forward on your efforts to improve your staff meetings. It sometimes can be a difficult and trying journey, but it is one that is equally rewarding and worth the extra effort you will need to put in to improve your group. We wish you the best as you take what you have learned here and begin to apply it in the real world. Enjoy the journey—your efforts will pay off as you move forward.

Bibliography

Dickman, M., Stanford-Blair, N., & Rosati-Bojar, A. (2004). *Leading with the brain in mind: 101 brain-compatible practices for leaders.* Thousand Oaks, CA: Corwin.

Doyle, M., & Straus, D. (1982). *How to make meetings work! The new interaction method.* New York: Berkley.

DuFour, R., & Eaker, R. (1998). *Professional learning communities at work: Best practices for enhancing student achievement.* Bloomington, IN: National Educational Service.

Eller, J. (2004). *Effective group facilitation in education: How to energize meetings and manage difficult groups.* Thousand Oaks, CA: Corwin.

Garmston, R., & Wellman, B. (1999). *The adaptive school: A sourcebook for developing collaborative groups.* Norwood, MA: Christopher-Gordon.

Goleman, D., Boyatzis, R., & McKee, A. (2002). *Primal leadership: Realizing the power of emotional intelligence.* Boston: Harvard Business School Press.

Hargrove, R. (1995). *Masterful coaching: Extraordinary results by impacting people and the way they think and work together.* San Diego, CA: Pfeiffer and Co.

Jackson, T. (1993). *Activities that teach.* Cedar City, UT: Red Rock.

Kuhn, T. (1996). *The structure of scientific revolutions* (3rd ed.). Chicago: University of Chicago Press.

Lipton, L., & Wellman, B. (1998). *Pathways to understanding: Patterns and practices in the learner-focused classroom.* Guilford, VT: Pathways.

Midura, D., & Glover, D. (1995). *More team-building challenges.* Champaign, IL: Human Kinetics.

Newstrom, J., & Scannell, E. (1998). *The big book of team-building games.* New York: McGraw-Hill.

Robbins, H., & Finley, M. (1995). *Why teams don't work: What went wrong and how to make it right.* Princeton, NJ: Peterson's/Pacesetter.

Rohnke, K., & Butler, S. (1995). *Quicksilver: Adventure games, initiative problems, trust activities, and a guide to effective leadership.* Dubuque, IA: Kendall/Hunt.

Senge, P., Ross, R., Kleiner, A., Roberts, C., & Smith, B. (1994). *The fifth discipline fieldbook: Strategies and tools for building a learning organization.* New York: Doubleday.

Index